# Beyond Beauty

# Beyond Beauty

## A Guide to Self-Love, Self-Confidence, and Full Feminine Power

ALEXANDRA VILLARROEL ABREGO

SelectBooks, Inc.

*New York*

This edition published by SelectBooks, Inc.
For information address SelectBooks, Inc., New York, New York.

First Edition

ISBN 978-1-59079-384-8

*Library of Congress Cataloging-in-Publication Data*

Names: Abrego, Alexandra Villarroel, author.
Title: Beyond beauty : a guide to self-love, self- confidence, and full
    feminine power / Alexandra Villarroel Abrego.
Description: First Edition. | New York : SelectBooks, Inc., 2017.
Identifiers: LCCN 2015040703 | ISBN 9781590793848 (pbk. : alk. paper)
Subjects: LCSH: Self-esteem. | Self-confidence. | Self-realization. |
    Femininity.
Classification: LCC BF697.5.S46 A27 2017 | DDC 155.3/3391--dc23 LC
record
available at http://lccn.loc.gov/2015040703

*Book design by Janice Benight*

Manufactured in the United States of America
10  9  8  7  6  5  4  3  2  1

# Contents

# Acknowledgments

The first thing I do when I wake up each morning, right after I open my eyes, is to say out loud, "Thank you!"

That "Thank you!" doesn't only go out to the universe and to God for allowing me to live my passion, but also goes to the people who encouraged me, supported me, and helped me all along this journey of making my dreams become true. To my friends and family who believed in me, and gave me the motivation to pursue my dreams. You all made this possible.

To my editor, my photographer, my amazing A.V.A. Dream Team and all the people who contributed in this project, a big Thank You for your outstanding work and for helping me meet my deadlines. I don't know what I would have done without all of you.

A special Thanks to Bill Gladstone, my literary agent who believed in me and this book from the moment we met, and who suggested the great subtitle: *A Guide to Self-Love, Confidence, and Full Feminine Power*, which he takes from his book *The Power of 12* where Gail, the main character, wrote a book called *Full Feminine Power*.

Another very special "Thank you" goes to my grandmother for always caring and always being so involved in my life throughout the years. You taught me so much about life and especially about self-love and self-respect. Today, I can't imagine how my life would have been if I had not had you there to guide me on the path of righteousness.

To my grandfather who passed away on May 11, 2010. You were and will always be the father that I never had. You passed on to me the love that you had for life, and for that I will be forever grateful. You are an admirable man who, until his last breath, showed so much strength. We all love you so much and truly miss you. May you rest in peace.

Now last but not least, I say "Thank you" to the most important and influential person in my life, my role model, my biggest fan, the person who folded me into the woman that I am today, and to whom I owe everything: my mother. She taught me everything I know and made me become the woman that I am today. I will never be capable of saying it enough, but "Thank you so much for being the protective and strict mother that you were and for now being my best friend. One life is not enough for me to give you back everything you gave me and to let you know how much I love you. Te Amo Mami!"

# Introduction

*As a girl, I did not know what I wanted to do,*
*but I knew the kind of woman I wanted to be.*

—DIANE VON FURSTENBERG
From her memoir, *The Woman I Wanted to Be*

When I wrote the first version of *Beyond Beauty*, I was nineteen years old. My initial goals were to sell a few copies of the book, gain credibility as a life coach, and, most importantly, earn the right to call myself an author. Little did I know that the words that I was writing when sitting alone at my local coffee shop, lying at night on my bed, or riding on the public bus, were going to be read by thousands of people around the world and would buy me a one way ticket to the life of my dreams.

After the book was first released back in October 2010, the orders slowly started to come in. At first, the book orders that I was receiving through my website were mostly local. Even back then, I remember how happy and excited I was just to think that people I didn't even know, and who didn't know me, were purchasing my dear creation; this was absolutely mind blowing to me. Then came American orders, then orders from France, Belgium, Algeria, Morocco, England, and many other countries worldwide. It was astonishing to think that people across the globe were reading my book. Soon enough, the book orders started to come every day, and my local post office became like my second home.

It's ironic to think that a simple idea can alter the course of your life forever, but it does, and I am a living testimony of it. *Beyond Beauty* quickly became a worldwide phenomenon. Without any television appearances, few radio interviews, and no media coverage, *Beyond Beauty* was selling like hotcakes. After two years of being a successful self-published author, I decided that it was time to take a more traditional route in order to share my message with a broader audience, and here we are now.

The initial goals I had to sell a few copies of the book, gain credibility as a life coach, and earn the right to call myself an author were all reached and then were exceeded beyond my wildest dreams. Today, my one and only goal and dream for *Beyond Beauty* is for it to become a movement and a manifesto for this generation of women. I want all women that read it to feel they are beyond beauty.

But what does being beyond beauty mean? I was often criticized for using this as the title of this book. For some people, "Beyond Beauty" sounded liked an arrogant and way too conceited title, as if I were calling myself someone who is beyond beauty. The reason behind my title choice is to urge all women to be beyond the image of just being beautiful. My wish for them is to unleash their inner and outer beauty shamelessly and courageously to become women beyond what society sees them as—the accessories and trophies of accomplished men. I want women to understand that they are valued beyond the appearance of their hair, body, clothes, and other attractive features. I want the modern women of this generation to look beyond themselves and search for a deeper meaning to life and existence. To do so, this book will take you on a journey of self-awakening and self-development where you will be taught to become your best self, create your dream life, and unleash your feminine power.

*Beyond Beauty* was created and structured in a way that will facilitate your learning and growing experience. It is designed in a way that allows women of this generation to improve each and every aspect of their lives, starting with their own selves, of course.

After reading all twelve chapters of this book, I want you to be able to proudly say: "I am Beyond Beauty." I want you to say it with pride and conviction, knowing that you have reached the point in your womanhood where you are beyond average or ordinary, a point where you have become an extraordinary woman, the one you always knew you could be.

Above all, you must understand that beyond yourself and beyond your life, there is a greater force and mission that unites us all, and when you go beyond who you are as a person and start living a life aligned with your purpose, that's when you become a blessing to the world rather than just a being with beautiful physical aspects or a being whose physical aspects are the most significant thing about you.

Lastly, I want you to understand that this is not just a book; it is a way of being for this generation. Humanity is going through a major crisis, where being feminine is looked down on, where beauty is artificial, where girls would rather be sexy than smart, and where women are ashamed of their nurturing nature. There has to be a change, and more than ever before we need to stand together in alliance to make this possible.

Times of crisis can also translate into times of change. We are living in an exciting, defining era at a time when there is a huge shift on its way. Actually, it's already here; it has arrived. We have entered the Aquarian Age, and at same time we are living in the Information Era. For the first time in the history of the world, with one simple click, we have access to the universe's most precious secrets and teachings.

Technology is one of the most powerful tools in the universe and if we use it in a way that can serve us and others, we are destined to awaken to the truth. I see it every day when people all over the world, from all walks of life, of all ages, are awakening and opening their eyes for the first time. It is our responsibility as women to help this shift come to its full fruition. We, the current generation of women, will either be the saviors of this world or the ones who sabotage our opportunities and our promise. Now is the time to teach our sisters, our mothers, our daughters, and ourselves to be Beyond Beauty.

# PART ONE

# Awakening

❧

*Awakening is the blossoming of the mind and of the spirit.*

—Venerable Wuling (Shi Wuling), *Path to Peace*

# 1

# A New Era

*Imagination is the beginning of creation.*
*You imagine what you desire; you will what you imagine;*
*and at last you create what you will.*

—GEORGE BERNARD SHAW, *The Serpent,* in Pt. I, Act I

## HITTING ROCK BOTTOM

When we think of beauty in this day and age, we very often associate it with superficiality. We think of a model on the cover of a magazine, or we think of all the cosmetic products that we have on our gift wish list, or we might feel a sense of resentment and anger from unhealed wounds associated with that word "beauty." All of these representations couldn't be farther from the experience of the meaning of true beauty. When I think of beauty, I think of the pure essence of a child, of the innocence in their eyes. I think of nature in all of its glory. I think of things that are far from a person being vain or superficial. This is beauty. However, I didn't always see it like that.

I believe that awakening to the truth starts the moment when we realize that we are the cocreators of our lives and our realities. Every thought and every action is molding our existence, and if we are not aware of this, we don't choose our thoughts and actions wisely, and as a result we won't create the circumstances and realities that we wish to experience.

It was in 2009 that I started to study and discover this truth. I was nineteen years old at the time, working a dead-end job. I always had too much month at the end of my money, as Jim Rohn would say. I was in an abusive relationship, and my weekends consisted of alcohol, parties, and melodrama. A year earlier I had moved into an apartment with a close friend of mine. She was a few months younger than me and we both wanted to be one of those strong, independent, and powerful women we saw on television on shows like *Sex and the City* or in music videos like "Miss Independent" from Ne-Yo. The problem was that we were just two young eighteen-year-old girls who had no money, no stable jobs, and, worst of all, no self-esteem. That caused us to believe all the propaganda we saw on television about what a good life is. We believed that living in a luxurious top-floor apartment with a fireplace, a Jacuzzi, expensive furniture, and a flat screen TV would make us happy, but it didn't.

One spring day in 2008 neither of us had any interesting plans in the afternoon, so we decided to get together and visit a few apartments available for rent in our neighborhood. We had previously discussed the possibility of leaving our parents' homes and moving in together, but it wasn't set in stone. That day, we completely fell in love with the third apartment we saw. It was located in a very central area, and the view was spectacular. There was a fireplace and Jacuzzi inside the two-bedroom apartment, and it was a top-floor corner unit. That same day, we signed the lease, and two months later we were both moving out of our parents' homes and into our very first apartment.

Obviously we had to make the decision to work full-time and forget about going back to school. Having chosen to live in luxury, we had to pay for it. I began working at a call center during the week and as a cashier at a pharmacy on weekends. It meant working at least sixty hours a week to afford the lifestyle we desired.

Our first year of living independently was great. We thought we had it all at the beginning, but we were so wrong. On the outside it may have looked like we did, but inside we were empty. Our top-floor apartment, the luxurious furniture, the designer clothes, the socialite parties on weekends, and all the other material things that I had in my life began to define my values and me. Today, I know and understand that it's the love that one has for oneself that defines us, not what we have or what we do to achieve success. However, I did not know that back then because I was too busy loving other people, and even worst, loving other things.

We live in a world that celebrates superficiality. Everywhere we turn, we are faced with false ideas of what happiness looks like. The private plane, the mansion, the Ferrari, and the public recognition are just some of the happiness and success symbols that are being programmed into our minds. I know that for me, at the age of eighteen, those external, materialistic luxuries were my ideals of success and happiness.

Everything started to change exactly one year after I moved into that apartment. I say "exactly" because that's literally what happened. The night we celebrated our one-year anniversary of living together, I went to bed in the early hours of the morning, and I had a dream that changed everything—a dream that moved me to a point where I began to change myself and, consequently, my life.

In that dream, I was all by myself walking in a dark alley. It was chilly and leaves were crumbling under my feet as I tried to walk quickly to get out of the alley. When I looked behind me I saw a man following me. He was dressed in a black suit and wearing a black trench coat. Every time I looked behind, he was getting closer and closer to me. Finally I stopped and turned around. He was right there. I looked at him dead in the eyes; he looked at me and said, "Come with me." I responded, "I can't. I have to stay," and that's when he said something that I will never forget.

He said "Why do you want to stay? Are you happy where you are?" In my dream, I remember wondering, am I really happy where I am? But before I could answer his question, I woke up.

As I looked around my beautiful bedroom, I gazed at the modern furniture, the designer clothes in my closet, the glass of wine sitting on my nightstand, and lying right next to me was a man that I was head over heels in love with. Yet I knew very well that he wasn't in love with me. I asked myself, "Am I happy where I am?" The answer was no. That morning, I opened my eyes to the reality of this for the first time.

That was the beginning of my awakening, the beginning of my creation. They say that hitting rock bottom is the best way to build and restart your life, because rock bottom is a great foundation for building a new life and a new self. I believe that to be true because that morning I had hit rock bottom and I had two choices, I could either stay on the ground devastated and defeated, feeling sorry for myself and simply continue to live the purposeless life that I had been living up to that point, or I could get up and start all over. That morning, as I saw myself hit my lowest point in life, I decided to pick myself back up and start all over.

## AWAKENING

When I first started to share that story in my talks in schools, organizations, and conferences, people would always come to me at the end of my presentation and ask me how I did this. They wanted to know what bridge had brought me from knowing that morning I had hit rock bottom to being where I am today. At first, I never knew how to answer. All I could think to say was that it is a process and that it took time, which is true, but I could see that my answer was never enough.

People like to hear specific events and moments that change others' lives; they like to draw a picture in their minds of what it was like—what it felt like, looked like, and sounded like. They want to perceive similar events and moments in their own lives so that they feel like they are on the right track themselves. So I thought back to what I remembered to find exactly what helped me or triggered me to want to make drastic life change after I woke up from that dream.

After that morning, I would spend a lot of time at home in bed, contemplating the lifestyle that I thought was so perfect. It was all make-believe, I had nothing valuable going on in my life. I was a nineteen-year-old girl working a full-time job that I despised. I was drowning in debt because I was always buying expensive things to impress people I sometimes didn't even like. The man I had in my life was treating me poorly, yet I wasn't strong enough mentally to leave him.

That whole superficial cover I had was bringing me to a point of exhaustion from pretending to be happy. I came to the realization that I was nothing like the apartment I was living in, beautiful inside and out. I was like many young women of my generation, beautiful on the outside, but on the inside so incredibly empty. I'm pretty sure you've already heard the expression "Looks can be deceiving," and it is true because you can be the most gorgeous woman on Earth and at the same time be very unhappy.

It was a hard time. I remember how my spirit was screaming that everything was wrong yet I didn't know how to make things right. I just wanted to get away and take some time for me, to "find myself." You know how people often take long trips around the world to "find themselves." But this is a waste of time and money if you ask me because if you are not happy with the person that you are, the person you are will follow you no matter where you decide to escape. I didn't know this back then.

One of my favorite Buddhist proverbs is: When the student is ready, the teacher shall appear. There is so much truth behind this saying. Everyone is on their own healing journey. We all have trials, lessons, and triumphs. For us to learn our lessons and afterwards triumph, the universe sends teachers, angels, and healers into our lives. People who you randomly meet—perhaps in an elevator, on a plane, in a park, or at the grocery store—are like shooting stars, bursting through your life, leaving a magnificent trail that changes the course of your path forever. Some of these teachers, angels, and healers stay longer than others, yet they are all as equality important.

⚬⌁⚭⌁⚭⌁⚬

Two months after I had my life-changing dream, I was working a late-night shift at my old dead-end job. When I finished, one of my colleagues, Baliq, offered to give me a ride back home, since I didn't own a car and it was late at night to take public transportation. We had been working together for over a year at that point, and though I didn't really know him personally, I knew everyone at work loved him. I felt comfortable accepting his kind offer.

Baliq was a few years older and a few inches shorter than me. You could see why everyone liked him. He was funny, smart, and charming. He would always pull out all of the stunts to charm the ladies, and he was the kind of guy most girls would see immediately as a friend.

That night, as he was driving me back home, we started conversing about life, the universe, and our goals and dreams. I was surprised to see how knowledgeable this man was about religions, metaphysics, astronomy, and spirituality. At some point during the conversation, he asked me how old I was; I told him I was nineteen. He stayed quiet for an instant, and then he began to mumble the numbers one and nine repeatedly. "One, nine, one, nine, one, nine," he was saying as he was driving and staring at the road. His left hand was moving in front of him from one side to the other and he looked at me and said, "One and nine are the two numbers of the infinite. After nine, we return to one. One and nine are two very powerful numbers when combined together. Everything that you will learn at nineteen years of age will change your life forever and will catapult you to your divine destiny."

I didn't know what to say or how to react to what he had just said. My cynical self wanted to laugh and think to myself that he was crazy, but something in me felt that I should believe what he had just told me and take it seriously.

We went on to talk about our past, and I asked him how he had gained all of his wisdom. He confessed to me that he had spent five years of his life in prison, and during that time he studied the Bible, the Qur'an, and the Buddhist holy books as well as metaphysics, numerology, astronomy, and other topics that helped him open his mind—what is known as the "third eye"—to the truths of our universe.

I did not ask him why he'd been sent to prison, as I knew that the man that was sitting next to me was a changed man, just like I was a changed woman. When he dropped me off at my home, it was cold and dark outside. But there was something different in the air that night, and I had a feeling of lust for life, of lust for truth, of lust for knowledge. I knew things were never going to be the same for me, and I knew very well what I was supposed to do from that moment on. I spent that year, when I was nineteen, studying ancient teachings, occult mysteries, laws of our universe, and secrets of the source, and as I did this, I began to awaken even more.

What is odd about that experience is that after that night, I never saw Baliq again. I heard that he got transferred to another department in the same building where I worked, but our paths never crossed again. I often asked myself if perhaps that night it was really an angel that I had encountered on my path. I rest assured that whether or not he was an angel, he certainly was a teacher. I, the student was ready, and he, the teacher, appeared.

Awakening or remembering, however you want to refer to it, are words to simply explain that all the knowledge of the universe is to be found within us. Everything we must know is already in the known world within us, which is why when we hear the truth, we recognize it, we applaud it, and we value it. Everything that I will share with you throughout this book is, deep down, what you already know.

Even though remembering and awakening are our principle tasks, we still have the ability and the power of creating—or co-creating, our existence and life.

## CO-CREATION

Creation is the first concept in the Bible. As a matter of fact, the first sentence in the New Testament is: "In the beginning, God created the heaven and the earth." Creating or co-creating yourself is a major step towards living the life of your dreams.

It is as simple as this: Before the nine months of pregnancy that your mother went through for you to come to life, she and your father had to first create you. Without the creation of you, of course, you wouldn't be here. Although your physical body was created many years ago, have you taken the time to create your life, your very own reality?

I remember the first time I heard the expression "Life isn't about finding yourself, it's about creating yourself." I couldn't really understand how you could create yourself. My mind was set up to think that one day, somehow, I would find who I truly was. So for years, I searched in vain. I looked in all of the wrong places: in relationships with men, seeking money and power, being over-involved with fashion and dressing well, and attending parties. Needless to say, I couldn't find myself, and the more I looked, the more I lost myself. It was like being lost in a forest by yourself. Chances are that the more you try to find your way out, the deeper and deeper into the forest you'll go, and the more lost you will become.

At nineteen years old, when I realized how deeply lost I was, my first instinct to try to find myself was to become a flight or cruise attendant. All I wanted was to get away, to travel and go to places that I'd never been before. Since I didn't have the money to do it, I thought that having a job like this would be the best solution.

So every day I was applying for jobs as a flight or cruise attendant. Becoming a flight or cruise attendant wasn't my dream career, but I thought that it was the most realistic choice I could make at that time, and it was the best way to escape my problems and worries. While looking for a job, I was spending more and more time by myself, and I started to read more and to write more to understand the reason why I was feeling the way I did. Without even realizing it, I was beginning my journey.

No matter how hard I prayed and hoped for an interview or job offer, none came. It's ironic how the universe operates and knows what is best for you, because only when I realized that what I needed to do was to create myself, I finally received a call from an airline company who wanted to hire me as a flight attendant. But by then, I was too busy creating the life I wanted, so I turned down the job offer.

You simply can't just "find yourself," no matter for how long you try. You can only create yourself and your future. If tomorrow you decide to stay in bed and not go to work, you can choose to do so. Of course you will have to deal with the consequences, but you have choices, daily choices that affect your future. Every choice and decision that you take today will have an impact on tomorrow, just like every choice and decision you took yesterday had an impact on today. You are the creator of your tomorrows, and one of the things that you can recreate or, shall I say, reinvent, whenever you wish to do so, is yourself and your life.

As women we have the power of creation. This is why we carry the children of the world in our womb. We have been chosen to create, which makes it easier for us, as women, to create our lives and our world. However, it's hard in the time we live in to stay still for a minute and think about what it is that we really desire out of life. It's difficult to understand our passion, purpose, and dreams, or even what we want to achieve or who we want to become.

For a long time, I allowed myself to be influenced by what others thought a young woman of my age was supposed to be. What we see on television—the glamorous people who display their money, beauty, and popularity—all of this was what I was aiming for while forgetting what really mattered was hidden behind all of that. What was inside of me is what needed the work.

## NEW BEGINNINGS

Every December 31, people all over the world get together to celebrate the coming of a new year, Since most of us are so caught up in the routines of our daily life, we seldom take the time to analyze what's preventing us from achieving our goals, or even to understand what it is that we want to achieve. But as we anticipate the possibility of a new beginning, we set the goals that we want to accomplish, and for many of us, it's a reason to try to improve ourselves, or to change and reinvent ourselves.

The celebration of the arrival of the new year then becomes the perfect occasion for millions of people around the world to decide to start all over again, to become who they really want to be and do what it is that they always have wanted to do. Yet only a small percentage of people follow their New Year's Day resolutions. The rest end up neglecting their goals shortly after the new year unfolds.

Even after the dream I had, and the profound revelation that I had the power to alter my circumstances, it still took me a while to start to radically change my life. But I believed my dream was a wakeup call, and it gave me the discipline to begin to change the habits of my daily routines and rituals. I began with small things, like not going to bed too late at night and staying home more frequently on the weekends instead of going out to parties. Then I made the bigger changes of reading more and writing more.

I was slowly aligning myself with the things that I wanted in life and with the person I wanted to be. I was basically, without really knowing it, beginning to recreate myself. Doing this takes time. I didn't wake up the next morning after my dream suddenly as a new person. Instead, I began a fascinating journey.

The mistake a lot of people make is thinking on the 31st of December a goal they have always wanted to achieve, such as "working out every day," is something they will have the capacity to make happen from sheer willpower.

But it's not like that. You need to patiently create new habits and beliefs and rituals. Step-by-step, you have to slowly let go of your old habits and align your life and yourself with the person that you want to become and the life that you want to have. If a drug addict decides that he no longer wants to consume drugs, he is not going to form a new way of living the day he stops using them. It's going to take time and effort and incredible persistence. More than anything, it will mean his making a dedication to a real commitment.

Don't wait for the 31st of December to decide to start living the life of your dreams. Now is the time to start creating the life you want.

Put first things first. Before thinking about going somewhere, you have to know where your starting point is, just like when you use a GPS. In order to get to a certain point in your life, let's call it the divine destiny, you have to know where it is that you are starting from.

## EXERCISE FOR EVALUATING
## TEN ASPECTS OF LIFE FULFILLMENT

There are ten aspects of living that define your level of fulfillment in life. I will tell you what these ten aspects are and describe what each one means. The only thing that you have to do is evaluate each one in your life. Be honest with yourself; this is fundamental.

Every aspect considered forms a slice of your life. When each is marked on a scale from 1 through 10 points, this leads to the possibility of a grand total of 100 points. If you measure yourself in this way, it will help you to gauge whether your life's fulfillment level is strong or weak.

The purpose of this exercise is certainly not to make you feel miserable. Please do not worry if you end up with a score of less than 50. It's not the end of the world. It just means that you have to work on a few things, and I will show you exactly what to do to get the highest score possible. It doesn't really matter what you get as a score now. Remember that much of the happiness and feelings of accomplishment occur while you are climbing the mountain, and not just when you reach the top. So here we go with the aspects to grade from 1 to 10 points. Just add your score number at the bottom of each aspect:

1. ***Your Emotional Health:*** This is not about your love life and how your relationship with your lover and good friends make you feel. This is only about you and your self-esteem, self-control, and self-love. What I mean by grading your emotional health includes asking yourself if you think before you act or speak, or are you generally impulsive? Are you capable of pulling yourself out of sadness and depression without the need for help from somebody else or substances such as prescription

drugs, alcohol, or stimulants and psychedelics? Are you in general a person who is confident and sure of yourself?

SCORE _____

2. ***Your Spiritual Health:*** This aspect of your life is not only about religion; you don't need to follow a certain organized religion to be spiritually connected. You can have a spiritual nature and not have any religious beliefs at all. This aspect of your life is about your values, your philosophical and ethical beliefs, and the integrity of your behavior.

> Do you take the time to sit alone in a room and listen to that voice within yourself?
>
> Do you believe that there is something more powerful than you that is in control?
>
> Do you live in the present moment?

SCORE _____

3. ***Your Social Support:*** Whenever something bad or sad occurs in your life, do you know that you have family and friends who are there for you? Do you feel like there are people around you that you can count on?

SCORE _____

4. ***Your Personal Growth:*** Are you always striving for more, seeking to educate yourself to have more knowledge for an even better future, or do you just live each day the same way and often settle for less than you are capable of?

SCORE _____

5. ***Your Loving Relationships:*** Do you have someone special in your life, someone with whom you feel a tremendous connection?

SCORE _____

6. ***Time Management and Organization:*** Are you frequently late? Do you feel like you are always running out of time? Do you keep on procrastinating when something important needs to be done? If you take a look at your bedroom or your home, is it usually a big mess? Basically, how organized are you in your professional life and in your personal life?

SCORE _____

7. ***Finances:*** Have you accumulated savings or property? Or do you live from pay check to pay check? Is your financial situation stable or is your credit maximized and money owed to others?

SCORE _____

8. ***Career and Profession:*** Is your current job on the path to your dream career? If not, are you at least doing something to get there, such as going to school or looking for a new job?

SCORE _____

9. ***Recreation:*** This is very important for each and every one of us and it is also very simple. Do you enjoy life? Do you do things that you like, such as going out, traveling, reading, or dancing? Whatever you enjoy doing as a hobby, are you taking the time to do it?

SCORE _____

10. **Physical Health:** Last but not least, how do you look and how do you feel? Are you in shape? Are you overweight or underweight? Do you eat what is considered a healthy diet? Are you regularly doing some form of exercise to be healthy instead of just sitting at your computer or watching TV?

SCORE _____

TOTAL SCORE FOR ASSESSING
EACH OF THE TEN ASPECTS THAT
FORM A SLICE OF YOUR LIFE: _____

Once you evaluate yourself by adding the points you give for each aspect, you'll know how you rank yourself overall, and also exactly which ones you need to work on. You should also set high goals for yourself in every aspect; these should be goals that go beyond your comfort zone. It is said that the people who fail are not the ones who aim too high, but rather the ones who aim too low.

You can repeat this test as many times as you wish. You could assess yourself every week or more or less frequently. What matters is to always strive for more, and then you'll receive a better score!

This can be the beginning of your road toward a better life and becoming a more happy and fulfilled woman. I'm going to take you on the same journey I've been through, and this starts by helping you to create the person that you want to be in order to live the life of your dreams. I titled this chapter "The New Era" not only because we have entered a new era globally and universally, but also because it is intended to be a beginning of a new time and new era for you.

I hope to contribute to your living the rest of your life in a more purposeful and meaningful way. You have the possibility of greatness within you. Although you may not yet have learned how to unleash your positive passions and convictions to have a life purpose, many things are possible. I am ending this chapter by sharing with you my favorite motivational quotation that I recite every morning. And now it's time for you to start doing the same. It's called "The Pledge to Success":

*"Today is a new day, a new beginning. It has been given to me as a gift. I can either use it or throw it away. What I do today will affect me tomorrow. I cannot blame anyone but myself if I do not succeed. I promise to use this day to the fullest by giving my best, realizing that it can never come back again. This is my life and I choose to make it a success."*

# 2

# Free to Be Feminine

*You can't separate peace from freedom because no one can be at peace unless he has his freedom.*

—MALCOLM X

Speech in New York City, January 7, 1965

*Malcolm X Speaks: Selected Speeches and Statements*

## WOMANHOOD YESTERDAY, WOMANHOOD TODAY

We are more free as women than we have ever been. Our great grandmothers never had the opportunities that we have today. Often they were discouraged from working and owning businesses and sometimes forbidden to choose their life partners. Many things were forced on them, and they didn't have many choices in life. Unfortunately, there are still some places in the world where severe injustice toward women occurs. While in most places women are freer than ever before, at the same time many are holding themselves captive. It seems as if after all those years of being imprisoned, the door opened, but we continued to stay with our back turned to the door because we were too busy pointing our fingers at men, telling them how it's all their fault. But is it really?

Men were not always on top; they were not always the strong sex, as a lot of people call them. As a matter of fact, there was a time when women were in power, where the female and what is considered feminine was worshipped and venerated. Way before us and our mothers and our grandmothers, and years before Jesus Christ, there was an era where the Goddess was supreme.

Now is a time of the return of the divine femininity and as it reemerges and rebirths into a collective consciousness, we are called upon in this period of awakening to free ourselves and our sisters from all limitations. To do so, we first must understand the universal shift that is happening in womanhood today.

◦✦◦✦◦

At the age of nineteen, when I started obsessively studying the laws of the universe, and studying history, ancient cultures, and other teachings, I began to discover that the state of womanhood today is deeply affected by our inability to let go of beliefs and ideas that we have been conditioned to accept—the ones that came with being born into the patriarchal society that we live in today. I understood at the time that if I really wanted to create myself, my life, and my future, I first had to free myself from all the negative beliefs that I had about being a woman. I had to first free the feminine within me.

Centuries ago the Goddess was acknowledged and worshipped at a time on planet Earth when women held higher power. There is evidence that proves that matriarchal societies once existed throughout the world. For the past five thousand years, we've been living in a patriarchal society, but before this happened, there were societies that valued women and worshipped Goddesses. Long before modern science existed and the human body was studied, women were thought of as mysterious beings because of their ability to birth children and sometimes were even considered to be superior to men. Later, when paternity and the cause of childbirth was understood, things began to change and we gradually entered the patriarchal society we know today.

Women began to lose their freedom and the respect for women's roles in society diminished. In only a few decades, women became an underclass that was not allowed to work, vote, or make decisions in their own community and homes, and the men began to dominate. Even though our mysterious life-giving power is no longer so mysterious, we still can bring a matriarchal society into today's world.

However, please don't get me wrong, this is not about diminishing the masculine energy, but is instead an attempt to elevate the feminine voice so that they can both become integrated and equal while remaining unique in their own strengths.

The first step is to understand what is going on in the world. Most of us are sleeping, conditioned to believe everything we see on television and read in the newspaper. In the first chapter of this book, I speak about awakening. Now is the time to wake up and realize that if we once were able to live and function successfully in a Goddess-worshipping society, it is possible to bring that mind-set and social order back. To do so, we must first allow ourselves to let go and heal from the past beliefs we have inherited. These are false beliefs that we have about our careers, our money, our looks, our relationships, our men, our worth, and everything else that our lives consist of. Those negative beliefs are holding us back from reaching our full potential and assisting this world into becoming a better place.

Our values about womanhood today need to return to what they were many centuries ago. We must be proud of our femininity and embrace our strengths and powers. It is the only way that we can free our sacred femininity, which is right now held captive under a cluster of lies, illusions, and false ideas. By bringing back the divinity of what is feminine, we will restore balance in the world. It is an exciting time indeed, and we are responsible for the possibility of this major shift. Before we go any further, you must understand that in order to change the world, you must first change yourself. All work begins on the inside, and for us to collectively free what is feminine, we have to first free ourselves.

In chapter 11, we will continue this imperative discussion about the feminine energy. Meanwhile, this chapter will teach you how to let go of all the negative, obstructive, and toxic ways—the beliefs, relationships, etc.—that are holding you back from reaching full freedom. Most of us like to believe that we are free. That's because when we are not in jail, in the middle of a civil war, or victims of kidnapping, we think we are free. But in reality, freedom is a state of mind. It is how you feel on the inside; your external world has little or nothing to do with it. You can feel free in jail. It is possible to feel free when enslaved. The fences of the mind are far more limiting than the fences of the earth. It's time to stop pretending and free yourself.

## OLD, LIMITING BELIEFS

Times have changed, but let's not forget that not long ago, women had to stay at home while men would go out in the world to provide for their family. These roles were the norm; they were rarely questioned or fought against, until one day women got up and decided that they, too, wanted to go out in the world and conquer what men had been conquering for centuries. They too wanted to work, make money, succeed, travel, and have the capacity to be independent. We sure have made it. We made our desires a reality but many of us have remained stuck with the old, limiting programming that was inflicted upon women for decades, and even centuries.

Although it was "inflicted" most women accepted this. It's time to take responsibility. Generation after generation, little girls in their mother's pearls watched daddy wake up in the morning, put a suit on or put on a pair of construction boots, and leave home to come back in the evening. They watched this, and somewhere inside questioned, "Why can't I do that?" It seemed more exciting and fun, not like Mommy's life, which was to stay at home, cook, clean, and take care of the children. Women accepted this for many years, simply because that's what they saw while growing up. Our grandmothers saw their mothers do it, the mothers of our grandmothers saw their mothers do it, and so on.

All those years of wanting to be like daddy created the deficit of feminine energy in our society today. The more women wanted to live in the masculine world, the more they lost their feminine side. They rejected the feminine and embraced only the masculine.

Even though the feminist movement in the in the early 1960s and 1970s (called "second-wave feminism" following the earlier movement of women's suffrage) accomplished a great deal of advances that now allow us to be free women, to be independent, and to be seen as leaders in the world, somewhere along the road women created or held onto old, limiting beliefs. These beliefs today are blocking us, keeping us from reaching our highest potential collectively and individually as women.

Those beliefs are that masculine is better than feminine— that whatever men do is somehow more exciting, important, and valuable than what women do. This belief that the masculine is superior and the feminine inferior is a belief that you must get rid of in order to free yourself and ultimately become a woman who goes "beyond beauty." Now let's discuss how we can eliminate an old and limiting belief.

Our mind is systematically programmed to remember past events, the emotions we felt when living them, and the physical reactions we had to them. If you had never felt what hot water feels like, you wouldn't know that hot water burns when you come in contact with it. We learn from our mistakes, right?

A portion of who you are is created by your belief system. If in the past you have only been with men who treated you poorly, you might be saying that "all men are dogs," but that is only because of your past negative experiences that you eventually turned into a belief, and that belief won't change unless you choose to change it. As human beings, we are more accustomed to experiencing failure than success: we have our heart broken many times before we experience true love, and when we are little, we fall many times before we learn how to walk. We also make poor decisions and mistakes that often lead us into failure and deception. Because of our lack of know-how, we settle for less so that we don't have to go through failure again. We become afraid of living fully.

Most beliefs that we have about life are created during childhood. It is at that time that our minds are absorbing everything we hear, see, and feel. It is only at around ten years of age that we develop our critical mind. Therefore, before that time, we don't have a filter, and we absorb and believe what is being said to us. If, perhaps, your parents made you feel like you were not good enough by always saying that you should be more like your older sister, later on in life this will create insecurities within you and a belief that no matter what you do, you are not good enough.

However, the good news is that most negative beliefs that we have are not based on something real and true, and can be destroyed and replaced by positive beliefs. We can replace our memories of past events with our imagination of what we believe is possible to happen in the future.

I want you to take the time to meditate on the beliefs that you have about love, money, work, womanhood, beauty, success, and yourself. Take a piece of paper and on different lines begin a sentence by writing "I believe . . ."

Here is an example:

I believe that love is . . .

I believe that money is . . .

I believe that work is . . .

I believe that womanhood is . . .

I believe that beauty is . . .

I believe that success is . . .

I believe I am . . .

By doing this exercise in an honest way, you will find what beliefs are hiding within you. Some you can keep—such as the positive, empowering, and uplifting ones—but some have to go. The negative, toxic, and destructive beliefs must be replaced by positive ones.

I remember a while ago having a conversation with a friend of the family. She is a young woman in her late twenties, and she discussed how she is no longer interested in dating or meeting men because all men are the same and have the same bad intentions. I was trying to explain to her that this is her reality because she has let it become her reality. She has been deceived in the past, and therefore she has created that negative belief inside of her, and because of that belief, she continues to attract men who have bad intentions. The power of our mind is incredibly strong, and when we believe something, it is manifested in our realm of reality. She admitted to having been deceived in the past more than once, and that because of it she had learned her lesson and wouldn't allow those same experiences to happen to her again.

This is a big mistake that people make, which is to believe that your lesson is a negative one. Whether it is that all men are the same, or that people are deceptive, or even that it's not good to take risks—beliefs like this hold you back and limit you, and therefore don't allow you to reach your full potential. What I said to her was, "The experiences and situations that we go through can at times be negative or positive. Life gives us difficult times and tests so that we learn great lessons. However, the lessons will always be positive. And if the lesson you have learned is not a positive one, you have not yet learned the real lesson. You still have to dig deep to see what the real lesson behind that experience was."

So always remember this through your evolutionary journey: All lessons are positive. Therefore any negative belief that you may have is a false one, it is an impostor trying to distract you from the real lesson that lies beneath, the one that will set you free.

## RELEASING AND RELINQUISHING

For the sake of expressing the idea of what occurs in a process of letting go and forgiveness, I like to think of "releasing" something as an outward action, while the "relinquishment" of something is an inner attitude. In the act of forgiveness release and relinquishment go together. How do you know if you have released or relinquished something? If you maintain an emotional investment in what you have let go of, you have not relinquished it. To truly let go of something, someone, or some place, you must both externally and internally let it go.

To free yourself, your mind, and your spirit from what is holding you back, you have to fully let go of all the baggage— whether it is the old limiting beliefs, destructive habits, certain toxic people in your life, or even material things and possessions that no longer serve your purpose. You can't move forward if you have a big wall made of bad memories and negative beliefs right in front of you obstructing you. What's incongruous about it is that we have built that wall. It is now up to us to destroy it.

We block ourselves from great things coming into our life because of the past failures, mistakes, poor decisions, and other negative experiences that we went through and never took the time to forgive ourselves for. When someone breaks your heart, for example, in order to be able to fully move on and forget the person, it is essential that you forgive them. Keeping records of "wrongs" will only harm you and create bitterness in your heart.

Like it or not, you are the one who has control over your life, so many of the past disappointments, heartbreaks, failures, and falls you experienced were caused by your poor decisions. Forgive yourself, figure out what the lesson was, and move on. Once you start to take responsibility for your life and for the consequences of your words, actions, choices, and decisions, you will then see how everything will start falling into place, and fall into peace.

Imagine that you want to wash the dishes but you can't because the sink is clogged. The memories of bad experiences, unforgiven mistakes, and negative people blocking you are like the dirt that is clogging the sink. Once you unclog it and throw the dirt away, the grimy water that is all the negativity and self-inflicted grief that you have in your life, will start draining away.

It all comes down to one fundamental thing—forgiveness of one's self. If you don't forgive yourself first, you will never be able to forgive others and therefore will never be free.

Forgiveness is never an easy thing to do, especially because most people think that it is a sign of weakness; but to the contrary, it is a sign of great strength. Our ego doesn't want us to forgive, because when we do, we slowly kill our ego.

The first step towards forgiveness is understanding. Understanding why you chose to do something that ended up hurting you. Or if you are trying to forgive someone else, understanding the reasons behind what that person did. What you will find will surprise you. Whenever someone hurts you, it is because they are mirroring their pain onto you. You can't hurt someone if you are not hurting yourself. The moment you understand the reason why someone wronged you, you will begin to feel compassion for them, which is the second step towards forgiveness. The easiest way to feel compassion for a person, no matter how evil that person may seem, is by seeing the child in them. See the lonely and hurt child that is screaming for love and doesn't know how to show it. The moment you begin to feel real compassion is when you begin to forgive. If you don't forgive first, there is no possible way that you will move forward.

Forgive your parents for what they did or didn't do. Forgive your past lovers for breaking your heart and leaving you behind. Forgive the friends who betrayed you. Forgive the teachers who couldn't understand you. Forgive the kids at school who made fun of you. Forgive the men throughout history who used, abused, and belittled you.

Forgive the women who saw it happen and didn't do anything to stop it. Forgive our ancestors for damaging planet Earth to a point where we have to worry about our children being able to swim in the ocean. Forgive the media that made you believe that makeup and hair is what makes you beautiful. Forgive humanity for the wars, the murders, the famine, the slavery, the poverty, and all the unjustified deaths. But above all, forgive yourself for what you did, when you didn't know.

Now repeat this affirmation: I forgive myself for all the poor decisions and choices I've made in the past. I forgive all the people who used me, mistreated me, and deceived me, and I forgive whoever wishes to see me fall and rejoice in my pain. I forgive the past and I set myself free.

Forgiveness is the key to releasing grievances, but most importantly in relinquishing them. Without forgiveness there can be no freedom. Without your freedom, you can't free the feminine.

## YOUR SURROUNDINGS

There is a story called "The Eagle and the Chickens" that my mother used to tell me when I was a little girl. The story is about an eagle egg that fell off its nest and was found by a farmer. The farmer brought the egg to his chicken farm where the eagle grew up with all the other chickens. The eagle was brought up by chickens to be a chicken, so he'd spend his days strutting around the chicken coop, pecking at the ground and acting like a chicken. The eagle believed that he was nothing more than a chicken, but deep down his spirit was crying out for more.

One day, he saw an older eagle flying in the sky. The old eagle approached the young eagle and asked him, "What are you doing among these chickens? You're an eagle, you don't belong on Earth. You belong in the skies."

The young eagle answered, "No, I am a chicken, and these are my brothers and sisters. I can't even fly."

The old eagle said before he left, "That's because you never tried."

The young eagle started to question himself and to wonder if it were true that he really was able to fly. He shared with his brothers and sisters that he felt as if he could fly and they all roared with laughter. "We are chickens, so are you," they said, "and chickens can't fly."

But one day, the eagle decided to try to fly. He jumped off a cliff, spread his wings, and soared through the sky.

The chickens looked at him with envy and then went back to the chicken coop where they belonged.

As you begin to awaken to your possibilities, you will notice that a lot of people around you, who are friends, family, or coworkers, will unintentionally start to resent you for it. They will begin to feel like they are losing you, as they see that you are changing, and this will create fear within them. They were used to the old you, and now that you are creating your new self. They are afraid of the unknown and also somewhat envious.

This is normal when all of a sudden you become the odd person who is trying to change and to better yourself. This does not mean that they don't love you or that they are bad people. Some people will at first be resistant to the new you, but with time, they will adjust and perhaps be inspired to also begin their own journey of awakening and ask you for help and guidance.

But if some relationships worsen to the point that they are negative or toxic it will be very difficult for you to reach your full potential.

In order for you to have a fresh new start, you have to get rid of baggage you have been carrying for years that is slowing you down. I'm not only talking about material things or beliefs. I'm also talking about a few people that are now in your life. Some people, who are not ready yet for this change, may continue being who they have always been with no desire to improve or change themselves. These are the energy drainers that at some point you might need to leave in the past. When you spend time with them, if they only talk about their problems and gossip about other people and the past, you will feel like they have sucked up all of your energy and that their negativity, just like polluted air, has invaded your body.

The more you surround yourself with people who empower and inspire you, the more you can grow beautifully.

Here's a little exercise. For every single relationship that you have in your life (family, friends, coworkers), ask yourself the following:

- *What is this relationship doing to help me become the best version of myself?*

If in answering this question you can't find at least one thing for each relationship, you must end it. As I said, you can't walk ahead if there is a wall blocking you. That wall can be made of people, of things, of past experiences or even regrets that you're still holding onto. But it doesn't matter how big that wall has become throughout the years, you still have the ability to knock it down.

Your associations have an enormous effect on who you are. There are confirmed statistics that the five people with whom you hang around the most have almost the same annual salary that you have, almost the same type of love relationship you have, and basically are living a similar type of life to the one you are living.

It's simple—do you want to have a healthy relationship with a man? Well, don't hang around only with single women! You want to be wealthy? Well, don't hang around with people who are broke and not doing anything to change their current situation. Imagine that an alcoholic one day wakes up and realizes that he is fed up of living his life the way he has lived it, and he wants to quit drinking. As much as this alcoholic wants to quit alcohol, recover, and be a better person, if he continues hanging around his alcoholic friends, there is little chance he will stop drinking.

There are some people in your life who, as much as you care for them, you know very well are not good for you. This is especially true in intimate relationships. One in every four women will experience domestic violence in her lifetime.

The moral of the story about the eagle and the chickens is that if you believe deep down that you can fly, you can't let anyone convince you otherwise. You have to spread your wings and leave behind anyone who is not supportive, who doesn't believe that you are a great person who can achieve whatever you put your mind to, or even worst, who is mistreating you. Sometimes you just have to let go of who you are with to become who you will be.

The same goes for dependent relationships. If you feel like your whole existence revolves around that one person and whenever he or she is not around you have nothing to do and feel helpless, that's not healthy, and deep down you know it. If you haven't found your life's purpose and you base your life on someone else's life, you will end up drained of all energy and strength. You can't take responsibility for someone else's life, but you can certainly take responsibility for yours.

Too many women are unhappy because of the man they have in their lives. Too many women spend their days focusing on trying to change a man more than they focus on themselves.

Some people won't change, but unfortunately not everyone understands or wants to understand this truth. I remember when, a few years ago, my grandfather was diagnosed with cancer. I used to visit him at the hospital almost every day before he passed away. There was a man in the room next to him who had just had an operation for lung cancer. He was a very nice man who made us laugh and liked to talk a lot. Yet every day, three times a day, he'd get up when he wasn't allowed to do so and go outside to smoke a cigarette. He had been a smoker for over twenty-five years, and even after two operations for lung cancer, he still wasn't ready to change and quit smoking. Why is that? It is because as I said, some people will simply never change. He is not going to change after the third surgery or the fourth or fifth. He is still going to go outside to smoke his cigarettes three times a day.

You can't afford to waste your energy and time on people who won't even help themselves. For example, imagine you are in the middle of the Atlantic Ocean at night and you are in a small boat with your lover. Your lover suddenly falls off the boat and you reach out your hand for him to grab it and help him get back on the boat, but he refuses to reach for your hand. The mistake that most women make is that they would jump in the water with their man because they'd think that they could save him. But the truth is that both of you would end up drowning. If someone doesn't want to participate in their own rescue, you can't allow yourself to drown with them.

Freeing yourself from toxic relationships is something that we all have to go through at some point in our lives. After our beliefs, relationships are the hardest things to let go of. This is because it involves another person, and of course we don't want to hurt their feelings. However, you must remember that relationships are here to serve us and not to destroy us. They are meant to help us grow and expand and not to hold us back.

The truth is that if you feel like someone is not contributing to your awakening journey, by letting them go (nicely of course) you are not only doing yourself a favor, but you are also doing the other person a favor. The new woman that you are slowly becoming will most likely not be accepted by the other person who is not ready for change. So is it better to let them go now than to wait for them to resent you and say to you the famous words anyone who has ever strived for a better life has heard, "You've changed. I liked the old you better!"

There are three categories of roadblocks:

1. The negative beliefs we have about different aspects of our lives. It is the first thing you have to take care of, and it can only be done by first realizing what those negative beliefs are, forgiving yourself and other people who inflicted them on you, and finally replacing negative beliefs with positive ones.

2. People who are harmful to you because they are not ready to grow and therefore want to keep you at their level. The relationships that you have with these people are destructive and are preventing you from becoming the greatest version of yourself.

3. Your physical surrounding, the things that block you physically from moving forward. Let's dive into that right now, shall we?

Take a look at your bedroom, your house, or the place where you spend most of your time. That place is a reflection of what your mind and your thoughts are like. If it's a mess, I'm sorry to say your life is probably a mess as well.

We are going to do what the opposite of the expression "inside out" means, by starting on the outside. Let's start by cleaning up the place where you live. Don't just organize the garbage—that doesn't count. You have to get into it, get deep into the action. Take every piece of clothing one by one out of your drawers and your closet and rearrange everything. Move every piece of furniture so that you make sure that you don't neglect the dust that hides under or behind your furniture. Get down on your knees and clean and scrub, just like Cinderella did. Oh, and remember that after all her struggles, Prince Charming came along, so just be patient!

While doing the big cleanup you will probably find some things that you no longer need and that are useless, but you're still holding onto, such as that pair of jeans that no longer fit or that empty bottle of perfume that you have had for a decade. Throw them away! You don't need them anymore. They are taking up unnecessary space that could actually be useful for new things. You have to let go of what is useless and negative so that there is place for the positive to come into your life.

Your surroundings must be an expression of the woman that you are trying to become. Make sure that you surround yourself with beauty, love, and femininity, and remember that your outside world is a reflection of your inner state. So yes, it is important to "clean up" your surroundings, but the most important work has to happen within. That is how you free yourself and ultimately free your inner femininity.

# 3
# A Woman's Value

*She is clothed with strength and dignity and laughs*
*without fear of the future.*

—Proverbs 31:25

## THE SACRED WOMB

We are Goddesses and we create life within us. We have the ability to carry a child in our womb for nine months and then deliver that creature to the world. Our womb is sacred. No matter what religion you practice or even if you don't have any religious beliefs at all, it does not change the fact that the woman's body was chosen to perform the most incredible miracle in the universe, the miracle of birthing a child and giving a human life to the world.

Why are our bodies, the woman's body, chosen to give life? Why were women chosen to perform this work? Why were our bodies equipped with the right mechanisms to perform such a beautiful act? Why were humans not born in the heart of a beautiful blooming flower? Or on the clouds, to afterwards be delivered by a stork? Or in the heart of the ocean? Or in the brilliance of a rare crystal or the core of an egg? Out of all the beauties that this world holds, it's within us that everything begins, that life starts. We were chosen.

We are blessed with the gift of creating and giving life. We hold an immense, irreplaceable, and valuable treasure within us. Yet we tend to forget about this.

Our bodies are sacred temples that we must honor. Even though we are more than our bodies, our bodies are the vehicles that we use to create life, beauty, and inspiration. Our body must be honored and when it is not, our value is negatively impacted. When the value of a woman is negatively impacted, so are the energies of the world. The masculine and feminine principles cannot live in harmony when a man or a woman doesn't respect the sacred space, which is the body and the life-giving womb.

When you are in tune with your worth and value, you respect the temple that is you, and you start becoming more careful who you allow to enter that temple. If you understand the power of your womb and your womanhood, you consider this before you let someone inside of you.

We hold the power of the universe—a power that exceeds all logic and science, a power that allows us to bring things from the unseen realm into the seen. Unfortunately, way too often in this day and age, we take it for granted, that gift, that mystery, and we allow any stranger to enter that sacred place, where only those worthy of feeling it, touching it, and being in it, should be allowed in.

To understand this is to understand how valuable your body is. When you value your body, you start being a lot more selective about who is allowed to enter and explore it. As Charlie Chaplin once wrote in a letter to his daughter, "Your naked body should belong only to those who fall in love with your naked soul."

Perhaps you have been conditioned to think in a "sexist" way about your body. You feel that nothing about your body is sacred because men feel this way, so you should think and behave as they do. We think that since some men, specifically those who are not in tune with their balanced masculine and feminine energies, sleep around, that we must do it as well—either because it's expected of us, or to please men. Women may feel pressured into making these choices, but that doesn't mean they are the right choices for *you*. If you know your own worth, you can make your own decisions without external expectations influencing you.

You might be resisting the idea of the sacred womb, but it is only by accepting the gifts and magical powers that you hold within that you will fully understand your value and worth. You will no longer want to be more like men. You will embrace your feminine essence, and you will see your body as being the temple that it is. You will know that only those who are worthy can have the privilege and honor of entering the center of creation.

If you ever feel worthless, remember that you are the mother of the universe. Your womb is where everything begins; your body is a sacred temple of creation and without you, human life on Earth would not exist.

## THE GENERATION OF SOCIAL DISRESPECT

I was watching an episode of *Iyanla: Fix My Life* the other day. I rarely watch television, but when I do, I only watch shows that teach me something. Otherwise I feel like I am wasting my time and I can't stand to do this, knowing how valuable and important my time is.

At one point during the show, Iyanla was speaking to a reality show star, a very sexy woman who was using her beauty and body to become financially successful and gain fame and popularity. She was all over social media posting revealing and provocative pictures of herself, leaving very little to the imagination. The reality show star in question did not see anything wrong with it, saying that it's part of our generation and that's what young women do these days. She stated, and I am paraphrasing, "Everyone does it."

Iyanla was trying to make her understand that the image that she was portraying to the world was conflicting with who she was trying to become. This woman claimed she was sick and tired of being mistreated and misused by men; she could not stand how they all saw her as nothing else but a piece of meat. She was tired of the humiliation and disrespect, not understanding that in a society where women are held to a double standard, those who play into a specific persona will be treated based on the image they present rather than who they really are. At some point, Iyanla said something that stayed with me, she said, "No, we don't live in the generation of social media, we live in the generation of social disrespect."

She is right. We unfortunately do. Social media has become a vehicle for social disrespect and you might not see it, until you learn about it; you might not understand it, until you grow out of it. Here's what I mean:

Social media started to explode during my late teens. I remember creating my Facebook account in my senior year of high school. Prior to that, I had profiles set up on a few other social media websites which were popular at the time, but sort of faded into the background with the arrival of the big players such as Facebook, Twitter, Instagram, only to name a few.

As I began experimenting with social media, I soon noticed how much attention you could get by simply posting a sexy picture of yourself on a social media website. The sexier, or should I say, the more revealing the picture, the more attention you would get. The more provocative the pose was, the more "likes" you would get. When you are still a young girl yearning for approval and acceptance, all that attention can become somewhat addictive. It can become some sort of drug that you consume and need in order to feel desirable and, even at times, beautiful. How sad is that? We live in a generation where the number of "likes" we get on a picture defines our level of self-confidence.

The problem is that most young women will rely on it to build their self-confidence, not realizing how wrong and harmful it can be. Your confidence should always be built from the attributes you have that can never be altered. Your body and face will change as you grow older, whether you like it or not. No matter how many shots of Botox you get, or how many plastic surgeries you go through, this is inevitable. It is the law of gravity in full action and no matter how hard you try, you cannot fight it.

It's time for women of Generation Y to start seeing their bodies as magnificent treasures that can only be discovered by those who are worthy. Understand that you don't need to become a sexual object to show the world that you are proud and comfortable in your sexuality. Sexual energy, which I will talk about later on in this book, is very important and it should never be something that you are ashamed or embarrassed of. It is okay to show that you are a sexual being, but don't let it define you and be the only thing people see in you. You are Beyond Beauty, beyond your body and looks. Your worth and value should never be defined by the size of your breasts or the curve of your back.

## RAISING YOUR STANDARDS

A woman's worth is immeasurable, it is all encompassing and everlasting. We are the mothers of this earth, the mothers of all humanity, inside of us is where all life begins. What a miracle that is. What a blessing we hold.

Unfortunately many young women in Generation Y are going through a major crisis because they are devalued. As we see this happen, instead of fighting it, we participate by putting a price tag on our worth. We accept money, luxury, and fame in exchange for our bodies, minds, and even spirits, thinking that our value is measurable, that it is exchangeable. What some young women don't understand is that our worth is priceless and timeless, our bodies, our minds, and our spirits should be regarded as treasures.

We must express what we believe our true value to be; we must show the world what we are capable of. If we don't show it, they won't know. If you go to a garage sale and see a beautiful painting, but no one is there to tell you how much it's worth, you might think that it is worth $100, not knowing that the painting is a very rare work of art done by a famous painter. In reality, the price is fifty times what you thought it was because you didn't know the value, the attributes, the rareness, the meaningfulness, and of course the worthiness of that painting. The painting was nonchalantly thrown on the dirty floor next to cheap and valueless items, in a place where almost everything sold is worthless and perhaps also useless. You never would have guessed how valuable that painting was because of how it was managed and carried. Yet its value remains and its worth prevails.

If you had seen that same painting hanging on a polished white wall of a prestigious art gallery with no dust or dirt on it, perhaps you would have seen its worth; you would have understood its value.

We are valuable regardless of where we are, what we look like, what we do, and how people treat us. No one can take your value away from you, but people might not understand your value and worth if you don't express it properly, if you don't show it or even know it yourself.

We need to tell the world how valuable we are. We need to tell them this by treating and seeing ourselves as valuable women. The way the world sees and treats you is a reflection of the way that you see and treat yourself, always remember that. Every decision you make, every word you say, every relationship you have, every job you take, is expressing your worth to the world. You are saying, "This is what I believe I deserve." Every time you settle for less in love, in your career, in your finances, in your everyday choices, you express your worth and value and consequently continue receiving more of what you have settled for.

Life will continue giving you similar results to what you are already getting until you raise the bar, until you raise your standards.

Just like the beautiful painting, you must find your way to the prestigious gallery to finally see what you are worth. To finally understand that your worth is immeasurable. To do that, it's your standards that you must to raise. If you continue settling for less, you stay in that same garage sale surrounded by worthless and undervalued items. There are three steps to raising your standards.

1. ***Believe in yourself:*** The first step is to believe that you are worthy. You must understand that you are a Goddess, a Queen, a rare and beautiful creation, and that without you there is no life. Always value your body, mind, and spirit, because if you don't, no one will—it is as simple as that.

2. ***Achieve valuable skills:*** The more achievements, knowledge, and education you have, the more you realize how worthy you are and your value increases. Obviously if a person spends seven years of his life studying to become a doctor and then graduates, he's not going to settle for a minimal wage job working at a coffee shop. He knows his worth and feels like he's earned the right to have an excellent career. He knows that he has the knowledge, expertise, and education to be a doctor and receive a good salary. If a person who has little education applies for a job offering a high salary, it's not logical to assume he might get it. Both of these people might be good people, with great hearts and who know that they are worthy of great things, but at the end of the day, if you don't have the achievements, knowledge, education,

and expertise to increase your value, it will be hard to get ahead.

3. ***Proclaim your value:*** Don't be ashamed, embarrassed or resistant to expressing what your standards are to the world. If you believe that you are worthy, and at the same time have achieved all that is needed to be achieved in order to receive what you want, don't be too shy to ask, whether it involves your job or a relationship. For example, it's your first date with a man that you like a lot but he is late. He said he was going to be there at 7:00 p.m., yet he shows up at 7:35 p.m. without even apologizing for his lateness. What most women would do in this situation is to just pretend that it doesn't matter and that they are "cool" with it.

   Why? Because they are afraid that it would be too much to show an attitude or to complain on the first date since they like that man so much that they don't want to scare him off. The problem is that if you give him a pass on being late once, he will probably be late every time because you have not set the bar high enough. You have not proclaimed your worth and your expectations. In any relationship, you need to show what your standards are from the very beginning and not be afraid to do so. If you want a man who is on time, tell him and don't feel bad about it.

I always say you can be the most gorgeous woman on Earth and still be treated poorly by men, society, and the world. Beauty is fleeting and deceitful. You can't always rely on that because, the truth is, it can be gone in the blink of an eye! You have to know what you can do that others can't do, what you know that others don't know. Your abilities, your good qualities, your skills, and your talents increase your value and make you become more valuable than others. In a generation and time when looks are so important to everyone, let's become a new breed of women, a new species, who goes beyond that. Being beyond beauty means being beyond the appearance of our hair, our curves, our eyes, and our smiles.

After you discover and comprehend what your value is, you may realize that your previous relationships in which you weren't treated the way you felt that you deserved to be treated, were failures not only because of the other person, but also because of you. You allowed him or her to treat you in a destructive way by staying in the relationship.

As women, we have to start taking responsibility for our own lives and removing ourselves from situations where we are mistreated. Of course, if a woman is trapped in a dangerous, abusive situation where great violence can occur, she must seek help. I am not implying that a victim of arbitrary violence should be blamed or made responsible for a terrible act toward her.

But in the realm of our "normal" relationships, if we stop allowing people to treat us disrespectfully, men will start to realize that this behavior is not acceptable. Generation Y women are setting the bar way too low and men don't feel challenged to be gentlemen. A woman who has self-respect always makes sure to demand respect from whoever approaches her. If people don't want to give her respect, she doesn't stick around. Why would she?

But young women these days seem to be afraid to demand respect and other things they are entitled to. They think that if they ask for too much, people will say they are divas or bossy, and call them some other sexist term. But as Madonna once said, "I'm tough, I'm ambitious, and I know exactly what I want. If that makes me a bitch, okay."

Knowing your worth in life or even in a relationship is fundamental because if you don't stand for something, they say you'll fall for anything. You have to know what it is you are bringing to the table and what it is you deserve, in love, at work or anywhere else. If you don't know your own value, how can you expect someone else to know?

## WOMEN AND MONEY

We can think of money as an energy, and this is why we call it currency. It does seem like a current, since it comes and goes and the beliefs that we have about money determine how much of it we have in our lives.

For centuries, women have been programmed to believe that money is not something for us to control, that men should be the primary breadwinners and investors.

I wasn't born into a wealthy family, so while I was growing up I was always told that you have to work hard to get what you want. Since I wanted a lot, I started working when I was fifteen years old. For years, I lived from paycheck to paycheck. I used to believe that life was actually meant to be that way. You work forty hours a week, eight hours a day, for an employer who pays you the minimum salary range until you're old enough to stop working. The mentality of the last few generations has been that you have to go to a good college, graduate with a respectable degree, then get a good job at a good company, and work for the rest of your days to be able to pay the rent or the mortgage. And if you're lucky enough to have a decent salary, you can buy the things that you want.

All these lessons we learned in the past affect our daily life, especially for women who, for centuries, were taught they should have less money than men and to depend on them for support. What I hope you and other young women can do from now on is not to be selfish but be "self-full." For women, this is often a difficult thing to do because of our nurturing side and our tendency to give to others. But if you give and never receive you will eventually become empty. Most divorces happen because the woman thinks she gives and never receives and doesn't feel appreciated and cherished. Don't get me wrong here! I am not suggesting to you to never care and never give—not at all. I am just asking you to sit down, be still, and ask yourself, "What about my life?"

Today, women are fortunate enough to have the right to work and go to school. We can now be self-sufficient without being judged. I know so many single mothers who are as successful as their male counterparts who are thirty-year-old bachelors who attended law school.

Many decades ago, if you were a married woman whose husband left you, you were considered a completely insignificant person. It was even worse if you were a widow, because your children were considered orphans because their father was dead, even though their mother was still alive. How lucky we are to live in this era and how very fortunate if we live in Westernized countries where fewer inequalities between men and women occur.

When women are financially empowered, the world becomes a better place. Children go to school and get the education they deserve, communities flourish, and social equality becomes a central focus. Women and money is a topic that needs to become a priority in the world today because even if we've come a long way, we still have a long road to travel.

Money and having value go hand in hand. How wealthy you are is often regarded as a representation of how worthy you are. Or should I say, of how worthy you realize you are. Your value to others will often translate into the amount of money that you make. The more valuable you are to the world, the more money comes into your life, and like a current, will increase its flow into your world when you increase your own value.

As women we have many walls to knock down before achieving financial freedom. The first one is to overcome some of the conditioned beliefs that we have about women and money. Maybe you've been raised in a household that believed that women should not make more money than men. Or perhaps you are afraid that your financial success could intimidate men and that because of it you will wind up alone. Those kinds of beliefs that you have about money must be destroyed in order for you to become financially free.

The second wall has to do with more precisely understanding that it is the value that you bring to the world that creates your ability to add wealth to your life. Think of people like Oprah Winfrey, Bill Gates, Richard Branson, and other wealthy people. They all somehow continually add their positive value to the world to create money in their life. In every industry, the person who adds the most value is usually the one that makes the most money. Therefore the secret to wealth is inside of you all along.

This is another reason why knowing your worth and understanding how valuable a woman you are is so important.

# 4

# Self-Confidence 101

*I am not afraid. I was born to do this.*

—JOAN OF ARC

## THE CHILD IN YOU

What if we are all born as confident beings? What if we all came to this world loving everything about ourselves—our skin, our smile, our body, our perfect imperfections. What if we came into the world whole and complete, but somewhere along the road, we changed and started to question if who we are is enough, if what we look like is someone beautiful.

If this was how we were born, we made the mistake to believe what the external world was telling us—which is to believe that we aren't at all perfect, when in reality, something of perfection is in each and every one of us.

While this image of how we think and feel when we are born is a fantasy, there are many things about this that correspond to the real feelings we have about ourselves as children.

Often as children we were never too shy, never too embarrassed, and never too resistant to show who we were. As toddlers, walking around naked was okay. Being the center of attention and showcasing our talents in front of family and friends was normal; it was something that we did without hesitation. Why hesitate when there is no self-doubt or fears? Why hesitate when we know that we are confident and feel perfect.

But then we started to grow and absorb the external thoughts, beliefs, and limitations of the world. We began to believe that who we were was not enough and that we needed to change ourselves to fit the mold. Slowly but inevitably our level of confidence started to lower until it hit the floor.

Perhaps it started the day your parents turned red when you came downstairs without your underwear or diapers on and told you that you should not do that again. It continued to lower when you wanted to go play outside after sunset and your parents didn't allow you, telling you that the outside world is dangerous. Your level of security decreased even more that day. A couple of years later, you started school and teachers told you that you had to have good grades to be smart; that didn't help. And as years passed by, you grew older and less confident. Perhaps you were rejected by the first boy you liked, or kids at school thought you dressed in a funny way, or you weren't great at sports. It all got worse when you started to be a media consumer—watching TV, reading magazines, listening to music. All the negative imagery impacted your level of confidence in terrible and devastating ways.

The child in you is bruised, afraid, alone, and confused. We all are, until we finally understand that feeling like we have beauty and perfection is our birthright. We are whole and complete as we are and there are no external factors—clothes, money, jewelry, hairstyles, fake tans, painful diets, or makeup brands—that can make us feel really good about ourselves. The hurt is deeply rooted within us from all these years of being told that a new outfit, a new hairstyle, or even plastic surgery, will make us feel confident.

Americans spend an estimated 33.3 billion dollars each year on cosmetics and other products meant for enhancing beauty.

Imagine what would happen if instead of spending this money on our vain desire for external beauty, we spent it on education. If we only educated ourselves and, more importantly, our daughters on how to really gain self-confidence, we wouldn't need external chemical products to feel better about ourselves. If we told them that self-confidence comes from within and can only be acquired and increased by what you know and what you do, not what you look like and how people see you, than maybe the sad child in us would heal.

The inner affirmations are what really matter. Outer affirmations are nothing but a false sense of who you are; they fade away, just like the makeup you wear. In this chapter, I am going to explain the difference between these kinds of affirmations and how you can become a more confident woman. You will soon understand that having confidence is merely a part of who you are, a part that somewhere along the road you lost or you forgot. I want to help you find it all over again.

## INNER AFFIRMATIONS

Most women want to change at least one aspect of their physical appearance. They believe that by changing how they look on the outside, they will become more confident and secure about themselves. Unfortunately, that's not the way it goes. There is a big misconception about where confidence comes from and how you can gain it. Most people think that if you look a certain way, act a certain way, or have a certain amount of money, you automatically have a high level of confidence. But confidence is not determined by your outer circumstances or even looks. Confidence is determined by what I like to call your "Inner Affirmations."

This is not to be confused with "Positive Affirmations," which a lot of people use to activate the law of attraction and change their perceptions of life. Inner Affirmations are different. They represent the inner conversation that we all have about our own selves. That inner conversation or voice can either be uplifting or destructive.

A destructive voice would sound a little something like this: "You can't do it, who do you think you are?" "Look at your thighs, they're way too big," "You are not that smart, why would they give you the job?" "She's way prettier than you; you stand no chance against her." As you notice, it is not very empowering, and as you can imagine, this doesn't help to increase your confidence. The problem is that most women have negative Inner Affirmations and a hostile voice in their head that plays nonstop like a broken record.

Positive Inner Affirmations, on the other hand, sound more like this: "You can do it, you can have it all," or "You are perfect and beautiful the way that you are." Or "You are smart and valuable, why would they not want to hire you?" or "You don't need to compare yourself to others; you are unique and precious." Your level of confidence rises when you have a positive inner conversation about yourself.

Rather than trying to find ways to boost your confidence, you need to focus on finding ways to change your inner affirmations from negative to positive. The reason I used the word "affirmation," is because that's exactly what it is. You are affirming these positive or negative ideas and comments about yourself. Soon enough, they start affecting your self-confidence and your life. The positive affirmations used by law of attraction practitioners resemble very much the inner affirmations that I speak about throughout this chapter.

The main difference between the two is that positive affirmations are usually forced and intentional. When you recite your positive affirmations, you do it by using the conscious mind. You do it consciously by telling yourself that it's time to repeat your daily positive affirmations. Being a law of attraction believer and practitioner myself, I use positive affirmations too. I write them down on small pieces of paper, which I hang in different places around my house. I have some on my fridge, some on my bathroom mirror, and even more on my work desk. Every time I pass near them, I intentionally read them out loud. To do so, I have to use my conscious mind. I consciously command myself to read the sentences on the paper and use my willpower that is located in my conscious mind to actually repeat them.

Inner Affirmations function differently. You don't need to think about it, or to use your willpower to hear that little voice in the back of your head telling you how bad or how great you are. The voice always comes uninvited, whether it is negative or positive. Your Inner Affirmations are different from regular, law of attraction, positive affirmations, because they come from your subconscious mind and not your conscious mind.

Let me explain. The mind is divided into two parts: the conscious and the subconscious. The conscious area only represents 10 percent of your mind; your subconscious area represents 90 percent. Your conscious mind has the ability to choose or reject thoughts or ideas. Your subconscious mind is a little more complex. It contains three areas: the critical area, the known zone, and the primitive mind. Formed around the age of seven to nine years old, depending on the child, the critical area of the subconscious mind is responsible for critical thinking and decision making. If you have children, younger cousins, or nephews, you have probably noticed this.

As the child approaches his tenth birthday, all of a sudden he realizes that Santa Claus does not exist. He no longer believes in every single thing that you say to him; he now has his own beliefs and opinions and makes his own decisions about what he wants to wear. With this development, the child can now filter what enters his known zone. He begins to choose which lessons, memories, and experiences he wants to keep in his mind. Before the critical zone is developed, the child has no power over what memories he retains. These memories will then affect his primitive mind, which is the way that he reacts to events in his life.

A good example for this would be: A child gets teased a lot at school by other kids. When he gets home, he goes to see his mother and cries in her arms. To console her boy, the mother bakes him his favorite cookies. Later when he grows up and becomes an adult, he may automatically feel the need to seek food when others tease him. It's going to be his way to escape, to ignore and not confront the problem head-on.

If you are not aware of how your mind works, you will be clueless as to how to change what goes on inside of you. For most people, their Inner Affirmations are based on what they heard or saw as children. If someone was rejected, abused, and victimized as a child, they will most probably have negative Inner Affirmations. Before the age of seven to nine years old, children don't have filters. They don't have a critical area that allows them to pick and choose what they want to believe and carry with them for the rest of their lives. Before that age, children are like sponges, absorbing everything that they are told. When your Inner Affirmations have been created by negative past situations, there are three steps that you must take:

1. Forgive whoever has hurt you or mistreated you.

2. Understand that what other people have put you through does not have to define the person that you are today.

3. Replace the old, negative, and destructive Inner Affirmation by a positive and empowering one.

For step number three, here is an example:

If you grew up being the "black sheep" of your family, and you were told repeatedly that you will never be as good as your older sister, today you probably have issues fitting in with social groups, issues with your self-worth, and you probably feel insecure around other women. Whenever a negative Inner Affirmation like, "You will never win against the other woman who applied for the new position who will definitely get it since she is way better than you," tries to creep up on you, you can switch the script by saying out loud, "I am more competent, capable, and interesting than the other people who applied for this position, I will definitely get it!" This comes down to law of attraction positive affirmations.

Remember, positive affirmations come from your conscious mind, but the reason many people choose to continuously repeat positive affirmations is because soon enough, they become part of your subconscious mind. In the same way that your Inner Affirmations of today were created by what you repeatedly experienced as a child, your Inner Affirmations of tomorrow can be created by what you repeatedly affirm today.

Another way to create your own positive Inner Affirmations is by expanding your knowledge, practicing your talents, and working on yourself. Inner Affirmations represent the things that you know to be true about yourself. If you have many negative Inner Affirmations about yourself, it is time to create positive ones. Try to think about the talents and abilities that you have, that you know that no matter what happens in life, nothing can take them away from you. Remember that, your level of confidence is not determined by how you look or act on the outside, or at least it shouldn't be. It is and should always be determined by the things that you know make you special and different. That is the real secret to confidence.

## OUTER AFFIRMATIONS

Outer Affirmations are also very different from positive law of attraction affirmations. Outer Affirmations represent what the outer world around you is affirming about who you are. Whether you receive insults or compliments, they represent anything and everything that people say about you. Not only this, but Outer Affirmations also represent your environment, your surroundings, and the things outside of yourself that you have no control over. Outer Affirmations can also affect your level of self-confidence when transformed into Inner Affirmation, but you should not allow them to do so.

When you first came into the world as a small and innocent baby, you obviously had no problems with self-confidence or self-esteem. You had no shame whatsoever over how your hair looked (if you had any), what clothes you wore (if you were wearing any), or even how smelly your diaper was. You were completely and fully secure in your own skin. But the world happened and later, as a child, you started to listen to what society had to say about you. You started to believe those who were telling you that you are inadequate, that you are not good enough, that you can't be loved if you don't look like the women on television, that you are not smart if you don't have good grades in school, and that your life is not as important as the lives of others. That's how most people, especially women, lose their confidence along the way. They start to believe all the Outer Affirmations and slowly convert them into Inner Affirmations.

Outer Affirmations are an illusion and a lie. Whether they are positive or negative, you should never pay attention to them or let them become your Inner Affirmations, and even less allow them to have an impact on your level of self-confidence. If a woman builds her confidence on her looks and on the compliments that she gets from the opposite sex, imagine what will happen to her sense of self-confidence the day that she looks in the mirror and no longer sees the flawless young woman that she once saw, or the day that heads stop turning and those compliments become less frequent. You can imagine that her level of self-confidence will be out the door. This happened because she built her confidence on Outer Affirmations and not on her positive Inner Affirmations and the things that she knows to be true about who she is.

The fact that 80 percent of plastic surgeries are done on women aged thirty-five and older shows that there is a fear of aging in our society. Women are clinging to their youth to slow down the inevitable aging process. They do this because most of their lives, they have relied on Outer Affirmations to feel secure about themselves. As they begin to age, Outer Affirmations begin to disappear and their sense of confidence fades away. In an attempt to hold onto those Outer Affirmations, they resort to anti-aging creams and lotions and plastic surgery, in addition to intensive and sometimes unhealthy diets. Because they depended on a self-confidence built on Outer Affirmations they haven't learned how to accept the natural and sometimes even beautiful aging process.

There are also negative Outer Affirmations. People who have low self-confidence will blame that on their distorted body images and on the opinions that other people have about them. As explained, once your critical mind is developed, you get to choose what you allow yourself to accept or believe. The problem is that most people are not aware of this power which lies within them. Most people go through life not knowing that they have power over that little voice inside of them. Not knowing that they can actually control it or even suppress it. They do not know that people's opinions of them do not have to become their reality.

## SELF-CONFIDENCE VERSUS SELF-ESTEEM

Most people think that self-confidence and self-esteem are the same. In actuality, they are not. One of the many benefits of speaking three languages is that I get to compare words and their definitions in Spanish, English, and French. Let's take self-esteem for example. In French it is *estime de soi*; in Spanish it is *autoestima*. When you write a letter to someone in English, you put at the beginning, "Dear . . ." and in Spanish it is "Estimado . . ." from the root word *estima*, which we also find in *autoestima*.

*Estima* means feeling appreciation and affection for someone and it is similar to many words, one of them being *amor*, which in English is "love." In English, the definition of "esteem" is respect and admiration. And finally in French, *estime* means having favorable feelings for a person or a thing and *estime* is also closely related to *amour*, which is "love" in English. We can thus come to the conclusion that esteem in some way is equal to love. When I hear self-esteem, I hear self-love. When I hear self-confidence, I hear self-security and self-assurance. In fact, the definition of self-confidence is: A feeling of trust in one's abilities, qualities, and judgment. As you can see, self-confidence and self-esteem are two very distinctively different terms.

Here is a recap on self-confidence. Self-confidence is created by your Inner Affirmations, which are ultimately the beliefs that you have about your own self. These Inner Affirmations can be negative or positive. If they are negative, you have the power to change them to positive and therefore increase your level of self-confidence. Once again, the definition of self-confidence is "A feeling of trust in one's abilities, qualities, and judgment." Nowhere in that definition does it say this feeling of trust in oneself is based on "liking the image of yourself that you see in the mirror."

When you have trust in your abilities, qualities, and judgments, how you look or how much money you have should not matter. It is the lack of abilities and qualities that creates a lack of self-confidence. Remember, it is called Inner Affirmations because it's about what is on the inside of you, not what is on the outside. If you rely on your Outer Affirmations, you are setting yourself up for failure. I already said it, but it is worth saying again—Outer Affirmations are an illusion. Everything that is on your outside will one day be gone and there is nothing that you can do about it. If you think that by superficially building your self-confidence you will be happier, think again, because inner beauty lasts much longer than outer beauty.

The process of loving yourself is a lot different and perhaps a little more complex. In the chapter "Loving Yourself," we will go more in depth into this important topic. One great way to understand the importance of self-esteem is to take a look at Maslow's famous theory. In his hierarchy of needs, he explains how as human beings we have many levels of needs, specifically five. Once a need is fulfilled, we go up to the higher level of the pyramid of needs. The highest level of the pyramid is the need for self-actualization, which is the pursuit of talent, creativity, fulfillment, personal development, and achievement. Most people never get to that level because they can't fulfill their other four needs, especially the need for self-esteem which comes right before the need for self-actualization. The pyramid of Maslow's theory shows us that without self-esteem, there can't be self-actualization. In order words, without self-love, there can't be self-fulfillment.

PART TWO

# Enlightenment

*Enlightenment is the journey back
from the head to the heart.*

—Ravi Shankar

# 5

# The Misinterpretation of Love

*Your task is not to seek for love, but merely to seek and find*
*all the barriers within yourself that you have built against it.*

—Helen Schucman, *A Course in Miracles*

## WHAT IS LOVE?

Love conquers all. It really does and once you understand this, you begin the process of relinquishment of fears. Contrary to what most people like to believe, hate is not the opposite of love. Fear is the opposite of love. Think of it this way: Love is the North Pole and fear is the South Pole; they both cannot come in contact, they cannot rejoin. When you live in fear, you cannot experience love in its truest, purest, and highest form, and the opposite is also true.

I believe that the word "love" is probably the most misunderstood word in the dictionary. People abuse it and misuse it on a daily basis. The act of loving doesn't hurt, betray, envy, or humiliate another beyond repair. It uplifts, rejoices, cares, and brings peace to the soul. It is an energy that creates feelings of joy in the world. Its level of vibrancy is so high and pure that it can heal and save us, spiritually, mentally, and even physically.

The greatest example of the emanation of love can be seen in a newborn child or even a toddler. If you really want to understand what love is and what it looks like, spend time with a young child. You will notice how carefree, happy, accepting, and nonjudgmental they are. When they enter a room, joy and light follows; that's the energy of love. They carry that energy within them and it touches everyone who comes near it. What's funny is that at the beginning of our lives, we were all toddlers and babies and therefore, we were all light and joy. So what happened? Where did our love go? Did we lose it, did it get stolen, or did we forget about it? Truthfully, it's a mix of all three.

The moment that we started to compare ourselves to others, judge ourselves or others, or wish that we had someone else's life, intelligence, or beauty is when we lost love. It was also stolen away from us every time our teachers told us that we had to have good grades in order to be considered a good enough person, or every time our parents warned us about the dangers of the outside world and instilled fear in our minds. We forgot, and we keep on forgetting about it every time we allow our ego to choose fear over love. Yet whatever is lost can be found; whatever is stolen can be recuperated, and whatever is forgotten, can be remembered.

Love has been misunderstood and abused by people for centuries. When I first started my career as a life coach, a lot of people began to give me the title and label of relationship expert. My very first on-line blog was called Dr. Love. I would get hundreds of relationship questions from women all over the world on a weekly basis, and I did my best to answer as many as I could. Shortly after that, I began writing a weekly column for the number one Hispanic newspaper in Montreal, the column was called Casos Del Corazon (cases of the heart). As you can imagine, this too was love and relationship oriented. After years of answering questions from my readers, on my online blog, and for the newspaper, I came to the realization that the issue is not that women and men don't know how to move on from a relationship, or how to get their partner to commit, or how to keep the passion in their relationship alive, or even how to communicate more efficiently.

None of these are the real problem. The real issue that lies behind all of that is simply that people don't know what love is. I'm serious! Most people are absolutely clueless about what real, unconditional, and sincere love is or how it feels, yet they claim they are in love. Everywhere, there are people in unhealthy relationships—relationships in which they spend most of their time angry and sad, and relationships in which insults are thrown at the other person on a regular basis. In fact some are relationships in which unfortunately two people stay together thinking that they love each other when all they do is express hate to each other.

For way too long, I thought that love was supposed to be painful and complicated, that it was absolutely normal for me to cry myself to sleep almost every night because of the person I was in love with.

Someone once said that love hurts. Well, let me tell you, the person who first said that was as clueless about what love is as are the people who now repeat that saying.

In my late teens and very early twenties, I allowed myself to be in relationships in which I would be abused mentally and even physically, often spending my nights awake waiting for a phone call from these people, and pretending that everything was okay when deep down I knew that it wasn't.

I did not know love back then. I did not know that love, contrary to what most people like to believe, is not a feeling—it is an energy. It is not something that is created in your life because of someone, but rather something that can be created in your life only by you.

Here is the thing: Media, Hollywood, and society in general mislead us to believe that love is something that only occurs when two people who are attracted to one another fall desperately captive of the overwhelming and all-encompassing feelings and emotions that pour into their hearts when chemistry happens, which they like to call love. Yet little does the world know that this is not love; it is lust. Lusting for someone or something is not always a bad thing. It can indeed have its good side, but we should never even dare to compare it with the greatness that is love.

What does this mean? If love is not lust and love is not an emotion or a feeling, and real love is not an experience that can only happen when two people connect, then what is love?

The truth is that love is a magnificent, ever existent, and powerful energy that is flowing out from within us at all times. That which allows us to feel this energy is our conscious decision to focus our attention on loving and positive experiences, thoughts, and feelings.

We all desire the experience of unconditional love. Many people spend a great deal of energy proving to themselves and others that they are deserving of this love. By doing that, however, they only learn to experience love conditionally, based on how our families and the culture at large express love. Most of us were not taught that we have the ability to go directly to the Source of love whenever we choose.

You may be wondering, "Where can I find the Source?" As surprising and simple as this may sound, it can only be found within you. We have come to this world with love and in love and our collective mission is to create more of that energy in the world—to spread vibrations and symphonies of love in a world so crowded with fear. At this present moment, the world lives in fear: we have forces fighting day and night to keep the vast majority of people's energies in a low frequency wave that is the frequency of fear. But our job is to transform and replace that energy with love.

That's what love is; it is the energy that will save humanity. Without it, we are all doomed, and the next generations will never see the light.

You weren't expecting this, were you? Perhaps, you were expecting me to write in detail about the love that a woman and man feel for one another. Perhaps you wanted me to talk about first dates and what to do when your partner doesn't want to commit in a serious relationship because that's what this world and this society sells to you: quick fixes. These are a short-term solution for a long-term detrimental situation. But all of those quick fixes and superficial advices are in vain. You will never be able to experience a healthy, loving relationship with a partner until you understand that they are not the ones bringing love into your life, you are the one creating it inside of you. Whether your partner is there or not, it doesn't matter. You don't need anyone else to feel love. You could be alone on a desert island and still be able to experience intense, real, and powerful feelings, thoughts, and emotions of love. Many don't want you to know this though because if you did know this truth, you wouldn't waste so much money on all of the Band-Aid solutions offered for singles and couples. You wouldn't feel empty and incomplete and find ways to fill the voids with vices and materialistic possessions. You would instead understand that no one can create or steal love from your life. Love is in you, love *is* you.

## LIVING A HIGH-FREQUENCY LIFE

When you live in love, all is well; when you live in fear, all is hell. The knowing of this truth allows you to be more receptive to love. You start looking, searching, yearning, wanting, and, at last, receiving love in your life.

I used to wonder why sometimes bad things happen to good people. I wondered why people who do good deeds in the world and who have never done anything bad or malicious in their lives, can somehow be punished and have, as a lot of people call it, "bad luck." I personally am not a believer of good or bad luck. I believe that "luck is what happens when preparation meets opportunity," as Oprah Winfrey once said. I do believe in being blessed though. I believe that you can be endowed with divine protection and be highly favored. Yet, I do not believe that people can be "unblessed" and therefore be highly disfavored and divinely unprotected. Those beliefs made it very difficult for me to understand how and why bad things can happen to good people.

I spent many years researching this, trying to understand how this can occur. Is it just the way life goes or it there something that happens, whether it be by metaphysical, religious, or scientific explanation? I could not rest until I could find the truth.

There is a famous quote that a lot of people attribute to Albert Einstein, even though there is no substantive evidence that he is the one who said it. Regardless of who it was, I find this quote to be very true. It goes like this, "Everything is energy and that's all there is to it. Match the frequency of the reality you want and you cannot help but get that reality. It can be no other way. This is not philosophy. This is physics."

I've read this quote over and over again, each time understanding it more and more. I believe this is the best explanation of the law of attraction and how it operates in our universe. We have to match the frequency of the reality that we wish to have and then we will get that reality. This means that if you live in a frequency of love, you will get high frequency results in your life, positive outcomes. However, if you live in the frequency of fear, you will get low-energy, negative outcomes.

It doesn't matter if you are a good or bad person, this is a law of the universe in full action and you cannot stop it. It is the same as if a person decides to jump off the thirtieth floor of a high-rise building into the nothing. It doesn't matter if he or she is a good or a bad person, they will inevitably and eventually hit the floor. It is the law of gravity in full force. The law of attraction works in similar ways. If you are living in the energy of fear, perhaps you feel emotions of anger, sadness, confusion, disconnection, and so forth, you are opening the door for more low frequency events to occur in your life. The same thing is true for living in love. When you live in love and feel love-based emotions such as joy, happiness, peace, etc., you are inviting more positivity into your life.

If I think about some of the "bad luck" events and situations that have happened to me in the past or some of the worst days I've been through in my life, I realize that before they occurred, somehow I was living in fear for a certain period of time. I was either angry at someone, sad because of something stupid, or maybe I was simply confused about life and felt anxious about my future, and all of a sudden something really bad happened. What I didn't know back then, is that I invited that event into my life and I would even dare to say that maybe I created it. My low frequency energy created that *thing* in my world.

When you feel low energy, fear-based, negative emotions and feelings, it creates events in your life that match that frequency. Your internal state dictates your external reality. You create the good and the bad that happens to you. Take responsibility for it.

Living at a high frequency, in other words, living in love, allows you to live a life of joy, peace, and contentment. It then becomes harder for bad situations to enter your reality because the energy of love creates a protective shield around you.

Look back on, let's say, the worst day of your life, at the worst thing that ever happened to you. Realize that before that day, before that event and situation happened, somehow you had fear-based emotions in you. It doesn't mean that you were depressed, always unhappy or angry at the world. It simply means that maybe you had a few negatives thoughts, maybe you said a few negative words. Whatever it was, you invited more fear in. Don't let it happen again.

Live always in love, create only high frequencies in your life. You can do this by thinking about positive moments that have happened to you in the past, positive and beautiful things that you have witnessed before. You can also listen to beautiful, positive, and lovely music—the kind of music that makes the soul feel good, that makes your heart smile. You can spend time in nature, which is love at its best. The beauty, the colors, and the pure smells will raise your frequency. Spending time with children and pets is a great way to feel love too, since they are sources of powerful love. All you need to do is to remember that love is everywhere. Especially in you.

The reason first loves are so intense, powerful, and unforgettable is that they are our first glimpse of remembrance of the love that we lost, long ago. All of a sudden this energy flows back into our lives as it tries to endlessly push aside our fears and take over the eternity of our being. First loves are like reminders of who we really are. We are love.

When we first experience it, nothing matters but the feeling that it creates in our world. All of a sudden, all is perfect; all is well. Regardless of how your first love might have ended, I want you to go back to the beautiful, joyful, and exciting feeling that it provoked within you when you first started to experience it.

Later on, if that first love story of yours ended, it was probably because of fear. You, or your significant other, allowed at the time a feeling of fear to take over. Fear-based emotions, such as jealousy or insecurity, took the relationship over and slowly destroyed it.

By living a high frequency life and living in the atmosphere of love, you are leaving the door open for great things, wonderful moments, and loving relationships to enter your reality.

## BEING LOVE

The biggest misinterpretation of love is when people see it as being only a feeling; they reduce it to a simple emotion. Love is everything. It is who we are and all that we ever hope to be. Later on, I will explain how our collective mission as human beings is to love. It is to create more love around and within us. The best way to feel love and live love, is by *being* love.

You must understand that all loves are the same: the love that you feel for yourself, your mother, your lover, your friend, or even your dog is the same. It is just combined with something else. For example, the love that you have for your lover and partner is combined with passion and sexual attraction, and perhaps friendship and compatibility. The love that you have for your mother is combined perhaps with respect, admiration, and gratefulness. There is only one love; it is the same all the time. We simply combine it with different elements, feelings, and emotions. No love is better, higher, or stronger than another one. It is the elements that are combined with love that define how intense that love will turn out to be.

To create love you have to *be* love, first. Remember, love is an energy, and when created, it fuels all the different kinds of love that exist in your life, including the most important one—the love that you have for yourself.

# 6

# Loving Yourself

*Don't forget to fall in love with yourself first.*
—CARRIE BRADSHAW, *Sex and the City*

## EGO LIES

In my late teens and early twenties, I would always proudly claim to love myself. I felt as though my level of confidence was always at its peak and, at times, making me a little conceited. But all of it was fleeting. It was a show that I was putting up to protect myself and to intimidate others. I used this to make believe that I was untouchable and unbreakable, even if deep down inside I was actually very fragile and insecure. We often do that; we build protective mechanisms to hide our insecurities.

There are some people who play the comedian card. They feel insecure about their looks or bodies so they always make fun and joke about themselves. It's their way to protect themselves. Others, and usually we see this in women who feel insecure and lack self-confidence, will be very promiscuous and give their bodies to any men. Once again, this is another defense mechanism, a way that some women use to protect themselves and hide their insecurities from others and sometimes even from themselves. My defense mechanism was to proclaim how much I was in love with myself and how confident in my own skin I was. It was a way for me to fool others, so that they would not see how insecure I really was. I had repeated and proclaimed my self-love for so long that I was actually starting to believe that I was confident and unconditionally loving myself. But I wasn't.

My lack of self-love at the time would not allow me to receive or even to give love to others. You can only give the love that you know, and I did not know love back then. As I said in the first chapter of this book, when a lesson is not learned and the universe knows that it's our time and that we are ready for it, it sends teachers into our lives to help us learn whatever truth needs to be taught. They come in many different forms and, at times, it's long after they have left and walked out of our lives that we understand the role that they came to play in our growing and learning journey.

Before I could even embark on a self-love and confidence-learning journey, I first had to realize how lacking I was in those areas. All those years, I had been faking it, and now I was ready to face my own demons. That's when a teacher came into my life.

We first met when collaborating on a project. He lived in Miami and I was living in Montreal. At first, we started meeting on Skype once a week to discuss the development of the project, then it became every three days, and next we were Skyping every day, and our conversations had grown beyond the project and were becoming more personal than professional. We both liked each other very much but the distance was obviously a problem.

After getting to know each other "virtually" for a few months, we decided that it was time to meet in person. I had to travel to Bolivia and the plane was making a pit stop at the Miami airport for a few hours, so we agreed to finally meet on that day. I remember how excited and happy I was. I sent him a message before leaving Montreal and when the plane landed in Miami, I felt like my heart was coming out of my chest. My hands were sweaty and I could hardly breathe. The anticipation was killing me. I walked out of the traveler zone and into the entrance of the airport and I sat on a chair. I waited and waited and waited . . . but there was nothing; he was nowhere in sight.

After about an hour of sitting alone at the airport in Miami, I decided to send him a text message asking him if he was still coming. Shortly after, he replied saying that he was not. I remember feeling embarrassed, humiliated, sad, angry, and confused. I sat there and cried, but in reality I wasn't the one crying, it was my ego. A little voice inside of me started saying things like: "He probably came and saw you from a distance and didn't like what he saw so he left," or "You are not good enough, which is why he didn't even bother to come." My insecurities were pouring out of me just like the tears that I was crying. Without asking him why he wasn't able to come to the airport, I replied to his text message by saying, "Don't ever contact me again," which was my ego trying to protect itself with pride and arrogance.

That experience showed me that I wasn't as confident and in love with myself as I had made believe I was. In reality, I was extremely insecure about myself and totally dependent on external affirmations to boost my confidence superficially.

That is one of the biggest problems that millennial women face in today's society—all those external, superficial, and false senses of self-love and self-confidence. They say that if you wear certain expensive clothes, you love yourself, that if your nails and hair are done, you love yourself, or that if you take dozens of "selfies" of yourself a day, you love yourself. All of it is false, and believing it, feeds your ego and forges narcissist tendencies. There is a difference between self-love and narcissism, there is a difference between self-love and pampering yourself, and as I previously said, there is even a difference between self-love and self-confidence. In this chapter, I want to focus on self-love, on how to love yourself.

It can be both easy and hard to learn how to love yourself. It can be easy because in reality, you are remembering how to love yourself, not really learning. Everything that we know or need to know is already within us; we hold all the knowledge of the universe inside of ourselves. Remembering is a process of putting all parts and pieces we have learned back together. That is what we do most of the time. Everything that resonated with you up to this point throughout this book is not new information—it is merely a glimpse of what you already know inside of you. Although it can be easy, as I said, it can also be hard because you will have to retrieve memories from decades ago, the memories of you as a child. A time when all and everything was love and fear was nonexistent.

So what happened? How did we lose our love?

It got lost every time our parents told us not to go outside at night because the world is dangerous. It got lost every time we watched images falsely portraying perfection in television and looked back at ourselves in judgment and disgust. It got lost every time we compared ourselves to other people's talents, abilities, and looks. We came to the world with unconditional love for ourselves but somewhere along the line, sometime during this human experience, we lost our love.

Now the question is, how can we bring it back? How can we love ourselves, just like we used to in our early years?

I often find the answers to life's big questions in nature. Nature is our best teacher. The seasons, the animal kingdom, the vegetation, and the weather are all teaching us valuable lessons, but we are often so busy and distracted by the noise that we don't stand still to listen and learn.

When it comes to self-love, nature shows us how the sun and the moon each illuminate us in their own ways without competing with one another. It also shows us how the rose and the tulip have their own respective beauties, and the rose is happy and satisfied being a rose and the tulip is satisfied being a tulip. They each have their own beauties and unique features. It also shows us how water and wind are each extremely powerful and can destroy everything in a second, yet are so vital and necessary to our survival. When they come together, they become invincible, so instead of envying their powers, they learn how to reunite. Nature loves itself. It is accepting, caring, protecting, and renewing. We can see this as seasons pass. Nature restores and re-creates itself with every season that comes, each having its own beauty. That is self-love, knowing that even when all leafs fall and everything seems to be cold and frozen, a new time will come and flowers will blossom and warmth will return. Self-love is all about knowing how to take care of yourself, in all aspects of who you are.

That day at the airport, after I got on the plane towards my destination, I decided I was tired of being the brokenhearted girl, and that all the drama that comes along with a lack of self-love, or with letting my ego take over, was now going to be part of the past. At that moment, I knew that it was time for me to put some sparks back in the most important and longest relationship that anyone goes through, which is the relationship that you have with yourself. You have to fall passionately, deeply in love with yourself before you can love anyone else.

I began then to spend more time alone with myself, to treat myself to do the things that I loved doing, and to listen to the voice within. And most importantly I made a commitment to myself, the commitment that I would never again hurt myself intentionally because really, that's what we do most of the time. We get into relationships or situations that we know will eventually hurt us, or, even worse, we are in relationships or situations where we constantly are getting hurt, but we don't do anything about it. We stay there hoping that the person we are with will change or that the situation will, when in reality it is you who needs the change and needs to learn how to say, "I love you but I love ME more. GOODBYE."

## BODY, MIND, AND SPIRIT

As I said in the fourth chapter of this book, self-esteem and self-confidence are two very different concepts, yet most people view them as being the same. The truth is that you can have self-esteem without having self-confidence, and vice versa. That being said, they both help and assist one another to reach higher levels.

Self-esteem refers to how you feel and how you treat yourself overall. It is, in other words, the level of love and esteem that you feel for yourself. The best example I can share with you is the love of a mother towards her child. She thinks her baby is the most beautiful, intelligent, and cute baby in the world, and she takes care of his physical needs such as feeding him, washing him, and taking care of his appearance and hygiene. She also takes care of his mental needs by sending him to school, reading books to him, and by trying to share knowledge about the small and big things in life. And finally, she also takes care of the spiritual needs of her child, by nurturing him with love, maybe by sharing her religious and spiritual beliefs with him, and perhaps by going to church, the temple, or the mosque with him.

They always say that a mother's love is the most real, the purest, and truest love of them all, which is why I always use it as an example in describing how self-love should be. If we can learn how to love ourselves the way a mother loves her child, our lives will flourish and reach levels of happiness beyond our wildest dreams.

As is often said, if your cup is not full, you cannot overflow the cups of others. In other words, if you are not properly and truly loving yourself, you cannot and will not be able to love anyone else, at least not the right way. To achieve self-love, real self-love, you must do as the mother of the baby does. You must take care of all of the aspects of your being—body, mind, and spirit.

In a society and a generation where we are constantly bombarded by false images of beauty, success, happiness, love, and especially self-love, it can be very easy to lose yourself and think that by simply taking care of a few aspects in your life you are loving yourself. But that is not how it works. If you only take care of the mind, for example, and you neglect the body and the spirit, you are not loving yourself. If you only take care of the body and you neglect the spirit and the mind, you are not loving yourself. If you only take care of the spirit and you neglect the body and the mind, you are not loving yourself.

You must absolutely and immediately balance all three. Imagine a triangle in your mind where on each extremity you have one of the three aspects: body, mind, and spirit. They are all interconnected and need one another to form this triangle of self-esteem, a triangle that when fully connected gives you the ability to love others the right way.

Very often, I see women looking for quick fixes for self-love. Like a drug they consume, they give themselves to men who make them feel like they are loved for a few moments or hours, a few days or a few months. But like any drug, after the high comes the crash. The withdrawal is so painful yet most women don't learn a lesson from this, and so they continue to experience the same situation over and over again, with the same man or perhaps different men who come into their lives to teach them that self-love can only be created by themselves. It cannot be transmitted by another party.

The crash and burn experience is inevitable because when someone comes into your life before you learn how to love yourself fully and purely, you are not showing that person how to love you. You can't teach if you haven't learned yet.

Learning how to love yourself, or, as it is more popularly said, learning how to increase your level of self-esteem, is simpler than you think. Yes, I said it! It's simpler than you think. We tend to overcomplicate things for no reason, as we have the false belief that all the important and major things that you must do in life have to be complicated. Contrary to that belief, most things that are of major importance are very simple because it is already in our nature and part of our human experience must-haves. As I said earlier, self-love and love in general is something that we were born with; therefore all we have to do is to remember it.

I see a lot of beautiful women take care of their body. They go to the nail salon every week and hair salon every two weeks, they always make sure that they have the right outfit for the right occasion, and their makeup collection is like one at a cosmetics counter. There is nothing wrong with pampering yourself. Actually it is a good thing, because when you pamper yourself, you take care of the body, so in our triangle of self-love, only two dimensions are left for you to attend to. The problem occurs when a woman only pays attention to her body, or even worse only pays attention to the outside of her body. If you are only paying attention to your physical appearance, yet you don't eat right and you smoke and drink often, we most certainly have a problem and that problem is called lack of self-love.

It takes more than a nice outfit and a vibrant red lipstick to take good care of your body. And then again, if you do really and fully take care of your body and your appearance, but also the last time you opened a book or went to church was five years ago, well this time we have a bigger problem.

For each dimension of the triangle of self-love, there are a variety of things that you can do to take care of these three aspects. Here are a few suggestions.

*Body:* Spend a day at a spa, eat organic food, stop eating fast-food, exercise every day, practice a sport, drink eight glasses of water a day, sleep properly every night, wear clothes that fit you and that make you feel and look good, have good hygiene, wear the right amount of makeup to accentuate the curves on your face (only if you enjoy wearing makeup, of course).

***Mind:*** Read at least two books every month, take courses, attend conferences and seminars, play games that stimulate your mind, surround yourself with people you can have great and enriching conversations with, learn a new word every day.

***Spirit:*** Go to your church or mosque or temple every week. Read spiritual books like the Bible, the Quran, *A Course in Miracles*, or others. Think about the love of others, and spend more time in nature, listen to positive and inspiring music, practice an art, dance, spend time with children, do yoga.

It is simple, it is easy, and it is possible. All you must do is make sure that every single day you do at least one thing for each dimensions of who you are—body, mind, and spirit. That is how you increase your self-esteem, and that is how you truly love yourself.

Don't let the media fool you. You don't need plastic surgery in order to love yourself, you don't need people's approval in order to love yourself, you don't need a lover or a partner in order to love yourself, you don't need an expensive and luxurious car in order to love yourself, and you don't need to be rich and famous in order to love yourself. You don't need anything but time and attention for your body, mind, and spirit to love yourself.

## THE MIRROR EFFECT

Look around you. Everything is a reflection of who you are, of what is within you. Your external reality is a constant mirror of your internal state. It's amazing, yet disturbing at the same time. What this means is that everything around you, where you live, how you live, the money you make, the relationships you have at work, and the relationships you have at home, are all reflecting what is going on inside of you. To some it might be a hard pill to swallow. If your relationships with people at work are toxic, negative, and unbearable, this means that somewhere inside of you, you are in conflict with your own self. If you make little money and you are constantly struggling to pay the bills at the end of the month, there is a lack of self-value and self-worth that you feel regarding your own self. If where you live is a mess, your mind is a mess as well. Everything is a mirror so look at the mirror and see what needs to be fixed, what needs to be healed.

It's mostly the relationships that you have with others that reflect the relationship that you have with yourself. Every single relationship shows a side of you, of how you feel about you and how you think about you. We are so quick to blame others for how they treat us, but in reality they are simply mirroring how we treat our own selves.

When you have an argument with your partner, you might think that this is not how you want things to be, that you don't want to be fighting and in tears. The truth is that you have created it, that this is exactly what you want and even need on a deeper level. Your ego will refuse to believe this but your inner self knows this to be true. There is something that must be healed within you, which is why this argument with your partner has come to the surface. It is a reflection of a conflict within, a conflict that you have with yourself, and the great universe is simply using your partner as a mirror so that you can see the flaw that awaits to be fixed. It is the same for your partner; he or she, as well, has a pain within that must be healed, and he has assisted you, as you have assisted him or her into the creation of this argument so that both of you can help one another in your path of growth.

Relationships are great mirrors, just like your physical body. The physical body reflects everything that goes on in the inner self. Every disease is a simple consequence of not listening to the inner self for too long, of ignoring what goes on in the inner body.

I have had psoriasis since I was nine years old. All my life they told me that it was an incurable skin disease, and all I could do was apply topical creams and lotions on my skin to alleviate the rashes. Most doctors never told me that the reason why I had those rashes was because of the types of food that I was eating and my levels of stress. They all simply said that it was hereditary and that there was nothing I could do about it.

In my early twenties, at a point of my life where my entire scalp was covered with psoriasis rashes and many parts of my body as well, I went to see a holistic doctor, and he was the one to explain that my psoriasis was simply a reflection of my internal state. The foods that I was eating, the alcohol that I was consuming, the stress, anxiety, and other things that I had inside of me were causing my psoriasis. It is only when I learned how to control my stress and anxiety and started eating healthy organic foods and stopped drinking hard alcohol that my psoriasis cleared up.

Once in a while when I get psoriasis rashes, it is an indicator that I am not taking care of my internal body and that I need to be more careful. That is why today I love my psoriasis, because it is like having an internal alarm that tells me when I need to be more careful to myself. Psoriasis, like any other disease or condition that exists such as arthritis, elevated cholesterol, diabetes, high blood pressure, and many more, are simply mirrors of our inner world. The inner self manifests itself into our external reality.

That's how it is when it comes to your relationships. When you have relationships that go sour, relationships that are toxic, relationships that are abusive, it is a reflection of your lack of love—the love that you have for your own self.

# 7

# Relationships

*Whatever relationships you have attracted in your life at this moment,*
*are precisely the ones you need in your life at this moment.*
*There is a hidden meaning behind all events,*
*and this hidden meaning is serving your own evolution.*

—DEEPAK CHOPRA
*The Seven Spiritual Laws of Success: A Practical Guide*
*to the Fulfillment of Your Dreams*

## ANGELS, TEACHERS, AND HEALERS

People come and go, seasons change, and we move forward. As we go along our path, we meet a lot of people. A number of them stay in our lives for a day, others for a month, some for a season, a few for a year, and even fewer for a lifetime. What they all have in common though, is that they all have a reason for entering our existence. Every encounter has its purpose. Every relationship has its mission.

Some people walk into your life to teach you a lesson and then have to leave. Others come in your life to heal you from past wounds and then they have to leave, too. And others are angels who come to guide you and help you get to where you need to go. These short but magical encounters are my favorite.

There are also the rare people who will walk into your life to stay because they bring something to your life that helps you and makes you become someone better each and every day. Some people call them the spiritual partners; to others they are known as soul mates. You both help and assist each other in growing and becoming your best selves. You teach them lessons and they do the same. You heal them and they heal you, and you guide them as they guide you as well. It's a blessing when your spiritual partner finds you; your spirit rejoices and knows right away why they have come.

A mistake that is often made is when you start to have expectations and make plans with someone for a lifetime who is not meant to stay and must eventually go. As I said, some people are simply supposed to come into your life to teach you only one lesson, or heal you from a past experience, or guide you to your next step and then they must leave. Only the lifetime people can and will stay.

When you finally understand this, relationships become easier. Your relationships become more freeing and simple. You let go, if someone has to go, without any bitterness or sadness because you know that their mission in your life has been accomplished. I have experienced all four relationships: the teacher relationship, the healer relationship, the angel relationship, and the lifetime relationship. They are all beautiful in their own ways. Here is how you can recognize them:

*Angels* Angels come into your life in the most unexpected ways—like shining stars in the darkest night. They often appear in moments when you feel lost and confused and are looking for answers to your questions. As soon as you are open to receiving guidance, to receiving knowledge and help, they appear in your life and give you a hint or a sign.

When we think of angels, we often think of supernatural beings or spirits, which they can be, but they can also manifest themselves in real human form.

Angels can guide and help you and can also protect and save you. Their passing in your life is often very short, but memorable.

**Teachers** We meet a lot of teachers in a lifetime. They enter our lives to sometimes stay for a month, a season, or a year but as soon as we learn the lesson they have come to teach us, they leave. Their passing from our lives can sometimes be very painful just like when you were in school and the lessons you had to learn were complicated and difficult. The lessons that the teaching relationships are meant to teach you are rarely easy but they are indeed necessary. They help you reach a higher level of awareness to eventually be able to reach enlightenment. When we don't learn the lesson, the teacher, or another one that carries the same lesson, might come back into your life over and over again.

**Healers** In my opinion, there is nothing more moving than experiencing a relationship with a healer. Healers come into your life to heal past wounds that are still open. They stay until you heal and then they leave. When they go what remains is a beautiful memory and a trail of love, compassion, and peace.

As you experience a healing relationship, at first it can be very difficult because past pains come to the surface. But slowly the long healing process begins and when it comes to an end, you experience overwhelming peace.

**Spiritual partners** And finally, the spiritual partners, as I mentioned before, come into your life and stay forever. They are your soul mates, the people who you connect with on a higher level and who help you grow and reach your highest self. Spiritual partner relationships are rare but when they happen, they change your world.

These four types of relationships are necessary to our growth, and that's really what relationships are all about. Relationships are not meant to complete us, as the expression "finding your better half" confuses us to believe. No, not at all, because the truth is that we are already whole and we don't need anyone else but ourselves to be complete. Relationships are simply evolutionary instruments that help us grow and eventually, in this lifetime or perhaps the next, reach enlightenment.

## BREAKING THE CIRCLE OF KARMA

I was raised by a single mother. I was five years old the last time I saw my father; he and my mother were never married. I grew up not having a male figure involved in my everyday life. My grandfather and uncle were a part of our lives, but of course neither could replace my real father. Nevertheless, I still had a great childhood, I can't complain about that.

When people asked me if I missed my dad, my answer was, "How can I miss something that I never had?" because I never knew and I will never know what it feels like to have a father in my family since he never lived with us. I met him when I was five years old because I used to ask my mother all the time who my daddy was. She tells me I used to look at photos and family albums and ask her, "Is he my dad?" which is when she decided to contact him and ask him if he would like to meet me.

⊙⌒⟡⌒⟡⌒⊙

When I was nineteen years old, my older cousin told me a story about an incident that occurred when I was a little girl. We went out for dinner one night, and as we always did, we started talking about all sorts of topics—life, love, the past, the future, the present. And as we were talking about past memories, we began talking about my father. My cousin and I have around a twelve-year age difference. When I was five years old, she was about seventeen years old. Therefore her memory of my father was much clearer than mine was. Also at that time, she, my two other cousins, and my aunt and uncle had immigrated to Canada and stayed for about a year at my mother's house until they found their own place. So my cousin, being the oldest, had met and still remembered my father very well.

That night, she shared with me a story of an event from my childhood that I had no memory of whatsoever. For a few months when I was five years old, Sunday was the day that my father was supposed to pick me up so that I could spend the day with him. My mother would dress me up, and my cousin said I was always very excited that I would soon see him. Then I would wait in the front of the house and sit there anxiously looking for him and waiting for him to come for hours and hours.

Most Sundays, however, it was the same story. I would wait for him and he would either never come that day or would finally come, but was very late. Apparently that charade lasted for only a few months before my mother decided that it was better for me to stop seeing my father because after sitting for hours in front of the door in my pretty little dress, my five-year-old self would realize that her father wasn't coming to pick her up. On most of these Sundays, I would start crying and ask my mom, "Why doesn't my daddy love me? Why isn't he coming?" As I said, I don't remember even a small portion of this but the day my cousin told me this story, important things about my life started to make sense.

That same night, after dinner with my cousin, I went back home to the apartment I was living in with my friend and I started to get ready for my date. The man I was in a relationship with at the time was coming over. I touched up my makeup, cleaned up my apartment, cooked him dinner, put on my prettiest outfit, and sat on the couch to wait for the man I had in my life. He was supposed to come over at 9:00 p.m. and it was already 10:00 p.m. I remember I wasn't even worried or wondering what could have happened because that's how it was all the time. He was always late.

Later on that night, he sent me a text message saying that he wasn't able to come because he was playing poker with his friends. As I sat there alone on the couch after I had prepared a meal for him and cleaned up the apartment and gotten all dolled up for him, I began to understand the impact that the relationship that I had with my father had on my relationships with the opposite sex.

Even though I didn't remember any of those Sundays when my father was late or didn't even show up, somehow in my subconscious mind they had affected me. As a young child I had a male figure in my life who was almost never there for me, always made me wait for him, and most of the time did not show up when a plan had been made to see him. And there I was, almost fifteen years later, with a man in my life who was rarely there for me, always made me wait for him, and most of the time wouldn't even show up.

That night everything became clearer, and I realized that I had to break the chain of events, because if I didn't, the same story would repeat itself again and again, if not with the same man, with other men I would encounter on my path.

"Residual behavior" is what this is called, and in spiritual terminology it can be explained as being stuck in the wheel of karma. Wheels represent cycles, and cycles represent the reality that is in the constant movement that is called time.

When you don't learn your lesson the first time around, that teacher will come back into your life and that's where a lot of people get confused. They start to believe that a person is a lifetime person for them. But the only reason this person is coming back into your life is that you have not yet learned your lesson.

Other times, a different person comes along and enters your life with the intention of teaching you the lessons you refused to learn in your previous relationship. For example, if a woman is in an abusive relationship and the relationship somehow comes to an end but she doesn't learn the lessons that were meant to be learned during that relationship, she is doomed to experience another abusive relationship until she learns her lessons. Perhaps the new man that comes into her life is completely different than the last one, but he will again be abusive, simply because she must learn her lessons in order to escape the wheel of karma.

When you are living the same experiences over and over again and it feels like you are turning in circles, stop yourself and ask: What lesson am I supposed to learn? Finding the answer to this question will set you free from painful relationships.

## HEALTHY RELATIONSHIPS

In chapter 5, I discussed how love is a frequency and not just a feeling. It is an energy that you can create in your life without the need of something or someone, and to create it in your life means that you are living a higher-frequency existence and therefore not allowing negative events to occur in your life. Now that you have not only learned, but have realized and understood that this is how our universe operates, what about learning how to feel love, how to enter that high energetic field and stay in it? In other words, learning how to live in love?

As I mentioned in the previous chapter, there are many small things that you can do to create the energy of love in your life, but before you even try to apply these small habits and tricks, you must first understand the basics of sharing love energy in your relationships.

Relationship love is very misunderstood. Way too often, we come to believe that the person we are with somehow belongs to us. We want to have them by our side, possess them, and we see them as being our other half. The issue with that is that nobody belongs to you—nobody is your possession. Believing that some-one is creates a lot of suffering, and therefore chases away love and replaces it with fear.

There are three fundamental qualities of healthy relation-ships, meaning the type of relationships that uplift you, inspire you, move you, and change you. Healthy relationships are com-posed of forgiveness and compassion for another, surrendering the need for control to liberate another, and, most importantly, having an attitude without pride and ego. When these combina-tions are existent in a loving relationship, everything else falls into place, and everything else is well.

## Forgiveness and Compassion

Forgiving thyself, forgiving others, and forgiving the past is essen-tial. Way too often, we enter new relationships with the unhealed energy of the past one, which is a recipe for major failure. Being stuck in the wheel of karma from not having forgiven whoever needs you to forgive them prevents real love from pouring out of you. Forgiveness is essential for creating love and experiencing a healthy relationship. Before you enter a relationship, ask yourself, who have I not forgiven yet? Seek it and forgive, set yourself free.

Forgiveness is also essential in the midst of a relationship. When your partner makes a mistake, learn how to forgive. As humans in this evolving universe, we are doomed to making mis-takes, which means that your partner will inevitably make a mis-take, so forgive him. Of course, make sure that your partner has learned the lesson because if he hasn't he will make the same mis-take over and over again. If the mistake made is too much for you to bear, and you know that you can't continue on with the relationship, be forgiving, but let the person go. Forgiving doesn't always mean that the person stays in your life after being for-given. Forgiving is simply setting yourself free from fear and let-ting love in again.

As you forgive, an essential step to achieving this state of forgiveness is compassion. When someone really hurts you, the only possible way to forgive them is through compassion. Understand that what the person did was all they knew at the time. If they acted in malicious ways and hurt you, realize that they did so simply because they are hurting themselves. Feel compassion for someone who is hurting on the inside and projects that hurt onto other. Feel compassion for the small child within the person who is in pain and afraid.

### Surrender and Liberation

As I said, believing that someone is yours is not healthy. Surrender of possession of someone and liberating someone is a demonstration of love. Love someone enough to know that no matter where they are, whether they are in another city, another country, another continent or perhaps, no longer in this world, you still love them. Being able to say, "Even though you cannot be with me right now, I still love you," is a liberating love, it is a surrendering of the flesh and connecting the spirit. We are all spiritual beings having a human experience, and the only real love is the one that connects the spirits and not the flesh.

Manipulation and mind games are so popular these days. People manipulate their way into the hearts of the object of their affection, not knowing that forced love is fake love. Only real love will last. They say that when you love something, you should set it free. If it comes back it's yours, and if it doesn't then it wasn't meant to be. That is true, that is love.

### Prideless and Egoless

Love doesn't have pride. It doesn't listen to the ego. For years, I used to operate in my relationships with my ego. I used to have so much pride, which was created by my fear of being left behind. I remember how afraid I was that I would one day be abandoned.

As I said, love liberates, it sets you free, it doesn't hold, bind or imprison. Love says, "If you have to go, go, I love you." That's love. It doesn't mean that you don't want to be with the person, of course you do. You'd love to have them next to you, feel their touch, kiss their lips, but if it's not possible at the moment, love understands.

Love without pride and ego is pure and peaceful. It doesn't hold grudges or a record of wrongs; it has dignity but not pride. Once you experience egoless love in a relationship, you finally see how insecurities, jealousy, and fears are simply illusions created by the ego.

If there is a perfect definition of truly loving relationships, I believe that it is this verse from the Bible (KJV) [1 Corinthians 13:4-8]:

> *"Love is patient, love is kind. It does not envy, it does not boast, it is not proud. It does not dishonor others, it is not self-seeking, it is not easily angered, it keeps no record of wrongs. Love does not delight in evil but rejoices with the truth. It always protects, always trusts, always hopes, always perseveres. Love never fails."*

It doesn't matter what religion you follow, or if you even follow a religion at all, I just want you to observe every word in this verse and explore explanations of this definition of what love is.

> *"Love is patient"*: When using the word "patient" it means being patient with someone and understanding that people learn and grow at their own pace. It also means two lovers will wait for one another if by any circumstances they are forced to be apart.

> *"Love is kind"*: means that true love is kind and is active in doing good. You can't love a person and be unkind to them. Unkindness is caused by fear; fear is the opposite of love.

*"It does not envy, it does not boast, it is not proud":* This means true love is not possessive, competitive, or jealous. Real love rejoices in someone else's success and achievements; it is glad for the other person. It also doesn't boast, meaning that it enjoys the beloved person's success and accomplishments just as much as the other person enjoys his own. Not being proud means that you are able to give yourself without holding back.

*"It does not seek to dishonor, it is not self-seeking:* Many people are in unhealthy relationships where they think that they are in love with the other person, but both parties frequently throw insults and disrespect one another. A person who truly loves would be absolutely offended to hear people say that this unhealthy relationship is what we call love, because it is far from it. Love is unselfish and a person who truly loves thinks about the other person's well-being just as much as he thinks about his own, knowing that at the end of the day, we are all one.

*"It is not easily angered, it keeps no record of wrongs":* When forgiving a partner for a mistake they did in the past, you have to fully forgive them. Most people will keep a record of wrongs when they should be erasing any resentments in order for there to be love.

*"Love does not delight in evil but rejoices with the truth":* True love always seeks for the truth and promotes good deeds. It does not find satisfaction in wronging the other person.

*"It always protects, always trusts, always perseveres":* There is no such thing as loving someone and not trusting the person. If you are in a relationship, trust is one of the main ingredients that will make that relationship work. Remember that every relationship is a mirror; therefore if you can't

trust your partner, in reality, you can't trust yourself. As for protecting, love always brings protection to the heart just as a parent who loves their children would protect them.

*"Love never fails"*: It cannot be clearer than that. Love always wins and whatever tries to come in between two people who truly feel love for one another will fail.

That's relationship love, so forget about everything you've heard in the past in regard to loving relationships. Forget about that dramatic soap opera that you watch which teaches you unhealthy and heartbreaking views on love. Forget about what is usually portrayed as love between two people in the media. When you love someone it is not supposed to hurt. When you love someone, laughter is supposed to be more frequent than tears, and happiness should always overcome sadness.

If you are in a relationship and the opposite is happening, maybe it's time for you to let go of that relationship. Then be certain you love yourself. Before getting involved with someone in a relationship, you have to fall passionately and madly in love with yourself.

The moment that you start loving yourself is the moment that you will find love. Or should I say, that then will be the time that relationship love will enter your life. When there is a lack of real self-love, the only relationships that will come into your life will be ones to teach you how to love yourself.

# 8

# The Goddess Within

*She slept with wolves without fear,*
*for the wolves knew a lion was among them.*

—R. M. DRAKE, Instagram poet

## THE INTUITIVE SELF

With the collective shift in consciousness that is occurring in the world right now, we are hearing the word "intuition" more and more frequently, whether in casual conversations between friends at cafes or on national talk show segments. In the dictionary, it is defined as: "The ability to understand something immediately, without the need for conscious reasoning," or "A thing that one knows or considers likely from instinctive feeling rather than conscious reasoning."

Intuition is often associated with women. It is said that women have their intuitive powers developed further than men do. In reality, it is not necessarily only women who have an easier ability to connect with their intuition. Since it is the feminine energy that taps into the intuition, a man who is in touch with his feminine side will have an easier ability to develop his intuition, and it is the same for women.

Intuition is something we all have inside of us, but it gets buried under all the false programming and conditioning of this world. In order to reconnect with our intuition, we must undo the wrong that has been done to the body, mind, and spirit. We have to clear the gateways to our intuitive self in order to allow our powers to return to us.

In each lifetime, the intuitive self helps you make the right decisions and leads you to green pastures. It is a feeling, and at times a voice within, that is purely based on love. Many people have asked me if the fearful voice within them was their intuition, and every time my answer is the same: When the voice is based on fear, it is your ego. When the voice is based on love, it is your intuition. We all have ego and intuition speaking to us at all times. The closer you are to enlightenment, the louder the intuitive voice is. The further you are from enlightenment, the louder the ego voice is. Reaching full enlightenment, which few people do in their lifetime, is when the voice of the ego has fully vanished.

When your intuitive connection is strong, your human experience becomes easier and less hectic. You don't feel confused, lost, or lonely because your intuition is there guiding you at all times. It's like knowing that there is someone right next to you holding your hand through the trials and the triumphs of life. Your intuition also helps you to develop greater spiritual abilities and open your third eye, to see the things that can't be seen by the rest.

I always say that there is a witch hiding inside of every woman. She has been persecuted, humiliated, and denied for way too long. Our psychic abilities are waiting to be unleashed, waiting to be explored. It is our responsibility to tap into our divine powers, especially the one of intuition, and in doing so, heal and help the world.

Here are some suggestions that you can do every day that will assist you in tapping into your intuitive self:

### Clear your mind

Clearing your mind from all the clutter, from all the noise, and from all the negativity is essential to getting in touch with your intuition. The intuitive self will not show up as long as there is chaos. I have briefly discussed this in chapter 2, "Free Feminine." As I said, you cannot move forward in your evolutionary path if you have a cluttered mind. Let go of all the negativity, the old toxic beliefs and destructive patterns, and allow the intuitive self to install itself within you.

## Meditate

Meditation is the key to having a great sense of intuition. Take the time to meditate every day, whether in the morning or at night. It is always better to meditate in times of quiet and peace, which is why I recommend morning or night. It is usually a time when everything is still and everyone is most likely sleeping, so you will be more likely not to be disturbed.

You can also create tools to help you in your meditation process, like an altar. An altar is a place where all your sacred and precious belongings are. It can be religious elements, like the cross of Jesus Christ, a rosary, or a figurine of Buddha. It can also be spiritual treasures, like crystals and pyramids, and other energy-filled items. Light some candles, burn some incense, and meditate in front of your altar, and you may also want to pray.

## Give gratitude

Praying is something I practice every night. My praying ritual consists of my giving thanks for all of my blessings. I also take the time, right before I pray, to write in my gratitude journal. A gratitude journal is a tool that you can use every night to write five things for which you are grateful. It can be anything—watching a beautiful sunset, receiving a compliment or giving one, having dinner with a long-lost friend, spending time with your family, being healthy. The smallest things can be written in your journal, as well as the bigger things in life, but simply make sure to write five things every night. In doing so, you will be encouraged every day to see the good in your days by looking for things that make you feel grateful. After I write the five things for which I am grateful, I pray and give thanks to God.

## Listen

Listening is so important when it comes to activating your psychic abilities and your intuition. Listen not only to what is said; listen also to the unsaid. The best place and time to listen is when you are in silence. Listen to the signs, to the stars, to the moon, to the sun. Listen where and when no one is listening. You'll be surprised by what you hear.

## Watch what enters your temple

Your body is your temple and what goes in it can affect tremendously your intuitive abilities. What you eat, what you hear, what you see, and what you feel affects the temple, either negatively or positively. Your five senses of sight, sound, taste, touch, and smell are the gateways and doors to your temple. What you receive from your five senses is constantly affecting your temple and therefore affecting your intuitive capacities.

I remember a while ago having a conversation with a friend of mine who is a spiritual healer. He was sharing with me the different foods and drinks that we absorb on a daily basis that close our third eye and make it harder for us to be connected to the Source. The thing that really stuck with me was toothpaste. We all use it twice and even sometimes three times a day, but the fluoride in the toothpaste is a toxic chemical that closes the third eye. In other words, it affects your intuitive abilities negatively.

The foods that we eat and the products that go inside or on our body determine the state of our well-being. Try eating plant-based organic foods as much as possible. And always be aware of what goes into and on your body because this determines more than just your physical health.

### *Stay grounded*

When you are not a woman who is a grounded person, meaning a basically emotionally stable and realistic person, you are not well connected to the Source. If you are not well connected to the Source, you cannot access your intuitive powers. When you worry too much about the future or the past, you are not well grounded. When you feel anxiety and fears, you are not well grounded. When you feel superior or inferior to others, you are not well grounded.

Other things like having vertigo and dizziness can also be signs of not being well grounded. I find that the best ways to ground myself are by being present, spending time in nature, and also literally being on the ground. Sitting and meditating on the floor and walking barefoot on the grass outside are great ways to ground yourself.

### *Read*

And last, the act of reading is nonnegotiable when it comes to connecting with your intuition. When I say reading, I am not referring to entertainment reading, which is always good, I am referring here to educational reading. Find books that will teach you about spirituality, intuition, the inner self, and the energies in this world. It is only through learning that one can truly master a subject, and if you want to have a great connection with your intuition, you must learn how to do so.

## THE FLOWING OF SEXUAL ENERGY

Intuition is not the only power that the Goddess holds. Sensuality and sexuality are also important aspects of the divine Goddess. We are sexual beings, and there is nothing wrong with that. Society has led us to believe that sexuality in women is something dirty that we should be ashamed of it. Just like our femininity, our sexuality is often a taboo subject. We have been told that women are not supposed to be sexual beings, that only men can be, when in fact, sensuality is an important aspect of the divine feminine. If we learn to tap into our sexuality the right way, and use it for a greater purpose rather than simple instinctive animal enjoyment, we will understand that sexual energy is a gift to mankind. It is actually the reason for mankind.

Creative energy is connected to sexual energy. If we understand sexual energy, we can use it to create not only life but other miracles. We can transform our raw sexual energy into a creative force. Napoleon Hill calls it sexual transmutation in his widely known best-selling book, *Think and Grow Rich*. He writes in the book, "Sex desire is the most powerful of human desires. When driven by this desire, men develop keenness of imagination, courage, willpower, persistence, and creative ability unknown to them at other times. So strong and impelling is the desire for sexual contact that men freely run the risk of life and reputation to indulge in it." That is the power that sexual energy has on humans, so imagine if you choose to take that energy and transmute it into a creative force for whatever you wish to do or have.

In order for the vast majority of the world to remain unexposed to its powers, human sexuality has often been suppressed. People might think that we live today in a hyper-sexualized society. However, the truth is that we live in a hyper-pornographic society where sexuality is often not valued and is frequently misunderstood. Ignorance on the subject had led us to believe that sexuality is associated only with the physical body, but sexuality is both of the mind and spirit.

If we learn how to take the energy that is forged when a sexual desire is perpetuated, and we use it to create our dreams and life desires, we can become unstoppable.

To transform sexual desire into a constructive creative force is a very easy concept to understand. It is basically the ability to not give in to the physical desire for human contact. The energy that flows in your body when sexually stimulated is an energy of creation, which is why it creates life. However, if you restrain yourself from the sexual act and use that energy to stimulate each of your senses, you will be able to create, not a child, but perhaps a piece of art, music, literature, poetry, or whatever other outlet you choose to express yourself in.

This obviously does not mean that you should refrain from sexual contact all the time. A sexual act, is an act of nature, and when you experience it with someone else, you are exchanging energies with that person, which is why you have to make sure that their energy is one that you want to share. Choose your sexual partner very carefully and know that sexual intercourse does not in itself solve all the needs for love or even sex.

The moment of orgasm is a very intimate moment that a woman should share with a beloved one. That special moment is the moment when you are the closest to God; it is the letting go of the ego. You unleash the Goddess within. The characteristics of an orgasm are joy, vulnerability, spontaneity, as well as a sense of timelessness. Such experience should only be shared with a person of trust and care. I believe that sexuality and love should go hand and hand, and that you should share that sacred moment with a person with whom you feel comfortable being the sexual Goddess that you have always meant to be. A Goddess who is not ashamed of her sexuality, her femininity, or her female cycles.

## THE FEMALE CYCLES

A woman's life is based around her menstrual cycle, whether she realizes it or not, and whether she pays attention to it or not.

Our emotions, our energy levels, our creativity, and many other aspects of our lives gravitate around our menstrual cycles. Being aware of this and understanding it gives us the opportunity to arrange our lives around our cycles and not go against our natural feminine design and flow.

Unfortunately, no one teaches us this precious, oh-so-needed information. Instead, we are taught to be ashamed of our menstruation, to be embarrassed by our monthly bleedings. There is no greater embarrassment for a woman than having a bloodstain on her clothes during her menstruation. When we talk about our menstruation to other females, we lower the tone of our voice, and to a lot of people, the simple thought of a woman's monthly bleeding creates a sense of disgust and discomfort. How ironic is it that we pay to watch movies where blood is shed senselessly, where destruction of life is promoted, yet a woman who bleeds monthly in the name of creating life is degraded and many times humiliated.

I remember my grandmother once told me how the first time she got her period, her mother slapped her. She was sixteen years old and noticed her underwear had stains of blood on them, and since no one ever talked to her about menstruation or womanhood, she got scared and went to ask her mother. But instead of receiving an explanation, she got a slap on the face with some insults. She never dared to ask anything about her monthly bleeding again and grew ashamed, resentful, and embarrassed of her menstruation. Not only back then, but still today, a woman's menstruation remains a taboo subject to many.

Besides our sex education classes in high school, which only covered the physical aspect of our bodies, we seldom received real teachings about our female cycles, or as I like to call them, our sacred cycles. Society puts an emphasis on the infamous premenstrual syndrome and then recommends putting women on pills and medication at a very young age to alleviate the negative symptoms that PMS provokes, as they try to make us believe. They warn everyone, especially men, that women become "bitchy," nagging, raging lunatics once a month, and that there's nothing anyone can do about it because that's the way that they are.

These are convenient mainstream lies and serve as a great source of humor about the failings of women, which we conform to. Little do we know that in actuality, PMS symptoms are warning signs and wakeup calls about the disconnected and repressed feelings that we experience during our cycle. It is a ringing alarm telling us that something has to change.

The problem is that we have been convinced that everything that we experience through our biology as women—our menstruation, pregnancy, childbirth, menopause, and so forth—are problems to be medically controlled by hormones, medication, and surgery. Those are the lies of the patriarchal society that we are living in today. When a woman is menstruating she refers to it as "having the curse." However, back when matriarchy ruled, women knew very well the power of their cycles and the blessings in their bleeding.

In his book *Blood Relations: Menstruation and the Origins of Culture*, anthropologist Chris Knight discusses the cultural significance of menstruation and says that many thousands of years before electricity was invented, women ovulated when the moon was full and bled when the moon was dark. The moon and the female cycles became synchronized because women sought to regulate their time of fertility. The men hunted according to the lunar calendar, leaving under a dark moon and returning in the light of the full moon to receive sexual rewards from women in exchange for the food provisions from their successful hunt. In this way their tribal rituals of feasting celebrated the break of the woman's "sex-strike" and the connection of the lunar and female cycles as well as the connection of the blood of the animals and of women's menstruation.

Tribal mythology of ancient societies even included men "stealing" women's magical menstrual powers during ceremonies of "male menstruation." The males justified usurping this power by claiming that females had stolen the power to menstruate from men.*

One of the aspects of the divine feminine in the mythology of cultures is the female's connection to the moon. The average menstrual cycle of a woman is twenty-eight days, which is almost the same as the lunation cycle. Perhaps artificial light, constant bright nights, and fast-paced lives have disrupted our natural synchrony with Grandmother Moon, as she was called in Native American Lakota culture.

Women such as Linda Crockett, author of *Healing Our Hormones, Healing Our Lives,* and Louise Lacey in her 1974 book *Lunaception,* have offered speculations of a scientific explanation for the relationship between menstruation and fertility and the light of the moon. For instance, it is proposed that the pituitary gland in our brain triggers hormone production which sends messages to our ovary to release an egg, and all of this could be affected by the amount of light our brain senses at night when we are asleep. At the point of most light in the night, during the full moon, could be the time when women ovulate.

Our menstruation cycles were not only synchronized with the moon cycles but also with each other. Females would bleed with the dark moon, preovulate with the waxing moon, ovulate with the full moon, and premenstruate with the waning moon.

In ancient cultures when women had not yet been conditioned to be ashamed of their cycles, each month all women in the same village would unite to bleed together in synchronicity, nurture each other, and rest and renew themselves. We know there were sacred rituals of menstruation in some Native American cultures

---

* For a wealth of information and his original theory of women's prominent and initiatory role in human culture and how the females in power were usurped by men, see renowned anthropologist Chris Knight's book *Blood Relations: Menstruation and the Origins of Culture* (Yale University Press, New Haven and London, 1991).

that both men and women were aware of and respected and valued highly. During their bleeding, women would go in "Red Tents" or "Moon Lodges" away from the noise of the village and gather inner wisdom to afterwards come back to their village with new and wise information that would help the entire community. The feminine wisdom was highly honored.

In recent times, studies have shown how our periods often synchronize with the women who are the closest to us.

It's a shame that we lost those beautiful ancient rituals. I believe that the state of this planet would be much different if we would continue paying more attention to our sacred cycles and to the feminine wisdom.

As women, we are very emotional beings, and contrary to what society tries to make us believe, it is actually a very good thing. It is a great power that is needed in this world, now more than ever. The problem is that our emotions change throughout our cycle and if we don't understand how to adapt our day-to-day life to the seasons of our sacred cycle, we will find ourselves lost in emotional roller coasters which can negatively affect our work, our moods, our creativity, but mostly our relationships. One of the biggest reasons why a relationship between a man and a woman ends up going sour is not necessarily because men don't understand women, and vice versa, but mostly because we don't understand ourselves and our cycles. Therefore our emotions go up and down and our relationships are impacted by this.

There is a legend that was told by the elders of Native American tribes that menstrual cycles were a gift from Grandmother Moon to all women to help them release the pains and burdens they carried for their children and men. It is true that our menses help us release not only the toxins in our bodies through our blood, but also emotions and other blockages which we hold inside of us.

Each quarter of your monthly cycle is an experience in itself, and when you know what to expect from it, you can adjust your life around it. Think of your menstrual cycle as an internal compass or alarm that tells you whether you should slow down, be creative, or reflect on your life, and so forth. Unfortunately, women are never told that they should pay careful attention to their cycles. Instead we are told to ignore them. Tampon commercials promise us that if we use their products, we won't even feel like we are having our period and we will completely forget about it. More and more young women are going on the pill to control their cycles, and, even worse for some, to stop their bleedings for months or even years in a row. But now the time has come for us women to stop ignoring our natural and sacred cycles and instead understand them and embrace them.

Our cycles are in four phases that are also like the earth's seasons:

MENSTRUATION~(days 1 to 7)
*Winter | Dark/New Moon | Crone*

PREOVULATION~(days 7 to 14)
*Spring | Waxing Moon | Maiden*

OVULATION (days 14 to 21)
*Summer | Full Moon | Mother*

PREMENSTRUATION (days 21 to 28)
*Autumn | Waning Moon*

First comes the phase that is like winter, bringing an inward energy. At this time we feel like being inside, secluded and hibernating and away from the cold. Then comes the phase that is like warm spring where we start wanting to go out in the world to explore it. It's a new beginning; everything is coming back to life and blossoming. Then in the ovulation phase there's summer when it's hot, and everyone is happy outside, enjoying the warm weather while it lasts and harvesting the fruits of their labor. Finally comes the autumn phase of premenstruation days, with its decline of energy. As we start to prepare for winter, we begin to dress with warmer clothes. We want to be inside more often and we watch the leaves fall and everything starts to get colder and colder.

Each week of our cycle is different and makes us feel different. Our energy levels, wants, and inclinations differ from one week to the other because of the cycle and transformation that is occurring inside of us. As women, every month we go through emotional and psychological changes of energy, whether we are aware of them or not. When we are not aware of them, we can't prepare for them just like when someone is not aware that the winter is coming, they won't harvest during the summer and prepare for the upcoming cold. Here is a description of each phase of your cycle that is approximately a week long:

## *Week 1: Menstruation*

A woman's cycle starts on the first day of her bleeding. This is the menstruation phase where through our blood and our spirit, we let go of everything that is no longer serving us. In this first week, we are quieter, retired from the world, or at least we wish we were. Our body and our spirits long to be alone and in retreat, which is why many times during our period, we create fights and arguments with people around us. This is our unconscious attempt to get away and be left alone. We are no longer interested in the outside world. The energy that rules this quarter of our cycle is like winter. Winter solstice is the darkest point of the year, and this is what menstruation feels like inside of us. We want to stay in and keep warm.

This is a time for reflecting, focusing on what is going on inside of us, and releasing old ways, beliefs, and attitudes in order to start our new cycle the right way. When we take the time to look after ourselves during this phase, we have a greater chance of having a positive spring and summer. Toward the end of this first week, we start to slowly peek back into the world. We can use this time to envision how we want the new cycle to go.

## Week 2: Preovulation

This is a time for creativity, as we slowly start to enter the summer energy. It is the suitable time to begin new projects, to be active and grow. The spring equinox is all about new growth. The animals are procreating, the daylight is coming back after a long winter, and the buds are opening. Many researches have shown that during this time of the month, women pay more attention to how they dress and are more flirtatious. As the ovulation phase approaches, our bodies are sending out messages and signals to the opposite sex about reproduction. This happens whether we are aware of it or not, whether we want to reproduce or not. This is a time of planning for the summer season.

## Week 3: Ovulation

This is the time for manifestation; we are fully ready to create. Just like during the ovulation period when we create life, we can also create projects and new ideas. Just as during the summer solstice, we feel more awake and alive. This is a time where we want to be around people and be social. Therefore use this third week of your cycle to go out, socialize, and meet new people. It's the perfect time for this and for working on projects and finishing them. The main purpose of this quarter of our cycle is to create, so make sure you create something that will make the autumn and winter season less dark and obscure.

## Week 4: Post-Ovulation

The last week of your cycle is when you reap what you sowed. It is like the harvest season. This will be a time of celebration or mourning, all depending on what you have created and accomplished during your cycle. It is during this phase that women suffer from premenstrual syndrome. Many women begin to feel depressed and sad and wonder why they are having this emotional response to events in their lives. This change in mood is thought to occur because the body is mourning the fact that it didn't conceive a child.

In nature, the menstrual cycle of a woman exists to procreate, when a woman's egg is not fertilized by a man's sperm, our body instinctively feels a sense of sadness and failure. This happens whether we were trying to conceive a child or not. The only way to avoid this PMS symptom is by using the creative energy to create other things, such as working on projects and establishing goals and dreams. During this time of the month, we also turn inward as we slow down in preparation for menstruation.

Understanding the phases of your cycle allows you to go with the flow—literally. I will share with you small things that you can do during each phase of your cycle to be more in tune with the energies that each brings.

### *Taking Care of Yourself During the Week of Menstruation*

During your menstruation, the best thing that you can do is to be alone and retreat from your busy life. As women we often have the role of taking care of everyone. This time of menstruation is when you have to take care of yourself. If your lifestyle doesn't allow you to get away for a few days, simply take an evening off and have a relaxing bath with candlelight and essential oils.

If you don't take some time off away from the world, you will become irritable and purposely create arguments with the people around you. This is done unconsciously by your spirit and body so that you can be alone. During this time of the month, you are releasing and letting go of old ways and old beliefs and attitudes, and therefore you need time to reflect on your life. Unfortunately, there is no place for Red Tents and Moon Lodges in today's society, where women can gather together away from the village and their men and children. I am a firm believer that the world would be a much better place if there were.

In Native American tradition, if you wanted to destroy a village, you simply destroyed the Moon Lodge or Red Tent because without this place of gathering for women to intuit what was coming and what to do next, the village could not survive.

Seeing how the world is slowly awakening and watching the feminine power reemerge in today's society, I believe that there will eventually be a return of the Moon Lodges and Red Tents, perhaps not in our generation but in our daughters' or granddaughters' time. I do hope so. In the meantime, what I urge women to do is to create their own Red Tent at home to have a place of quiet and retreat where you can meditate and focus on what you want to let go of with your blood each cycle. A Red Tent is constituted of red linens, red stones and crystals, and red walls, if possible, to honor the color of our sacred blood.

During this time of the month, you can also wear red garnets to resonate with your physical experience. Use only red towels and change your bed sheets to red hue colors.

Back when women would gather in the Moon Lodges, they would bleed onto the ground to connect with Mother Earth. Today, this is almost impossible to do. However, some women still execute this ritual by collecting their blood in cloths, soaking it in water and returning it to the earth. They place it in their garden, backyard, and sometimes they have a special blood rose on which they pour their blood, and it helps it to grow beautifully. You can try this ritual each month and you will experience a great connection with Mother Earth, which transmutes everything that returns to her.

Your blood is very sacred; it is the source of life and during your monthly bleeding your connection with your higher self is greater. This is why during your menses, you feel more tired; it is your body's way to get you to sleep and have premonitory dreams.

Hindu women of ancient India understood the belief in the sacred power of creation contained in menstrual blood very well. Studies of ceremonies in ancient India conclude that the red dot (called the bindi) between their eyes was painted with menstrual blood. This symbolized the power to awaken and open the third eye and access ancient knowledge.*

Remember that your menstruation is a sacred time where you connect with yourself as well as your higher self. It is time to take good care of yourself.

### Best Activities during Week 2 of Preovulation

This time of the month is perfect for being creative and starting something new, in terms of projects, ideas, or goals. During this time of the month, begin new projects since they will have more chances of coming to fruition.

### Best Ways to Use Your Energies during Week 3 of Ovulation

This is the peak creative time for a woman. The same way that we create life, we can create other beautiful and magical things. However, this is not a time for starting something new. It is a time for working on what you have started in week 2 or finishing it.

During this phase of your cycle, go out, socialize, and surround yourself with people, your energies are at its peak so make sure you take full advantage of that.

### Reflections and Preparations during Week 4 of Premenstruation

This is the time for celebrating or mourning. This week is a result of week 1, 2, and 3. If you follow the instructions and advice I shared with you for each phase of your cycle, week 4 will be a

---

* For more information about the taboos and myths of menstruation, go to the following link of the project Mythri established by the Health Department and the Education Department of Karnataka, India, to educate young women about menstruation: https://mythrispeaks.wordpress.com/2014/03/26/menstrual-taboos-and-ancient-wisdom/

time of celebration. If you did not create something positive during week 2 and 3 and did not take time to retreat and take care of yourself during week 1, you will experience many PMS symptoms such as sadness, frustration, and depression.

If you went with the flow and you listened to your cycle, no PMS symptoms will be experienced.

During this quarter of your cycle, you are also preparing for your retreat time, for your menstruation. What you can do is cook ahead, change your sheets to red, prepare your red tent, etc. At this time, begin to imagine and envision how you want your new cycle to go.

If you begin to listen to your cycles and to arrange your life around them, you will notice the major positive impact that it has on your life and on yourself. The problem is that no girl is taught this as she grows into womanhood. Therefore every month, as she feels her emotions going up and down, she feels helpless and out of control and ends up believing what society is telling her: That women are crazy and overly emotional beings. She then defines her womanhood in those terms and unsurprisingly yearns to be cooler, calmer, and more collected like men are, and then grows ashamed of her femininity.

Without understanding our natural and sacred cycles, each month we hysterically embark on emotional roller coasters and extreme mood swings. A woman's emotions are real and powerful, and if we don't know how and why they are showing up, we cannot accommodate them. We cannot work with them.

## BLOSSOMING INTO A QUEEN

Some say that you become a woman after you first get your period. Others may say that you become a woman when you lose your virginity. Some others might say that you become a woman when you reach a certain age, such as eighteen.

I say that becoming a woman is much more than just having a hormonal change in your body, or blowing out a certain number of candles on your cake. Being a woman is a way of thinking, a way of being. There are many "women" who still have the mentality of thirteen-year-old girls, when their actual age is twice that.

We all come to the world as princesses of the great universe and as time goes by, we become queens of the world. However, to become a queen, you must go through trials and triumphs and you must understand the powers that are within you and use them wisely. You have to pass the tests of time and learn how to control the emotional rivers that flow throughout your mind and spirit. The queen has to earn her crown and has to work for her throne.

As Marianne Williamson said so eloquently in *A Woman's Worth*, "A queen is wise. She has earned her serenity, not having had it bestowed on her but having passed her tests. She has suffered and grown more beautiful because of it. She has proved she can hold her kingdom together. She has become its vision. She cares deeply about something bigger than herself. She rules with authentic power."

It is no coincidence that in the game of chess the queen always protects the king. We have in our spirit a shielding power that is gained through our suffering and our glory. If you are reading this, chances are you have been through hell and back, you have hit rock bottom and got back up, and you have been torn apart and were left alone to put the pieces of your complex puzzle back together. That's our strength and our suffering, and our glory is the reward of our dark nights.

A glorious time is coming for us women. We have been oppressed for so long, but we are slowly awakening to our powers and we are beginning to embrace them. It is the return of the Goddess. We are returning in full force, with more enchantment, tenderness, compassion, love, caring, and sensuality than ever before.

During the witch hunts of Salem and Europe, our great-grand-mothers and great-great-grandmothers were burned and brutally murdered because they expressed their powers and used them for healing and the salvation of our earth. But those times are gone. We are no longer afraid. Deep down we are all witches, wise women, and natural healers, just like our ancestors. And the patriarchy fears that—it fears the feminine. Being a witch has been associated with Satan and evil for way too long, but women who were called witches worshipped nature, and their purpose was to heal the earth, not to harm it. Because they did not conform to the ruling patriarchy they were slaughtered. It is crucial that we reclaim ourselves and the divine Goddess within us all.

Our powers can be developed and tapped into, but we first need to blossom into the queens that we were born to be. A queen is strong. She is never insecure, she is always noble and under-stands her emotions and expresses them with calmness and dig-nity. She is not reactive. She is proactive, and she knows how to rule over the throne using her feminine essence combined with the strategies of an ancient and wise warrior.

It is only by reclaiming our femininity, by creating a potent inner self, and by understanding that this human experience is not about you, but about something greater than you, that you will deserve the crown.

They are waiting for us to be ready—the crown, the throne, the castle, and the king. It is only when the queen is ready that the king will appear. It is only when the princess has grown into a queen, that she will be able to create her queendom.

PART THREE

# Self-Realization

*You had the power all along, my dear.*
*You just had to learn it for yourself.*

—Glinda the Good Witch, from the *Wizard of Oz*

# 9

# *Purposeful Living*

*Everybody is a genius. But if you judge a fish by its ability to climb a tree, it will live its whole life believing that it is stupid.*

—A POPULAR ALLEGORY

## FINDING A PERSONAL MISSION

*I* don't believe in coincidences, especially not when it comes to us and our lives. I always say: "Your existence is not a coincidence." I strongly believe that you are here for a reason, a specific mission that was assigned to you and only you. No one else has the ability to fulfill your life's mission for you or to play the role that you were given to play, and if you don't listen to the calling, you will deprive the world of your gifts and contributions. You will forever be a thief, stealing from the world your potential greatness.

I came to this realization one morning in 2009. Right after I had that dream, the question, "Am I happy where I am?" kept resonating in my mind. And even though I knew very well what the answer was, I was still in denial, believing that I was eventually going to feel better and that things were going to improve on their own. I was still in a state of not knowing that I had to be the one to make the change.

Every morning I would wake up at 4:00 a.m. to get ready for work and take the first bus at 5:23 a.m. I had to make three transfers for my commute that would take over one and a half hours. Every morning, I had to start work at 7:00 a.m. There was nothing different about my routine on one particular morning I remember well. It was cold and still dark outside, and I was yearning for the cup of coffee I would get during my transfer from the first bus to the second at a Tim Hortons nearby.

I was sitting in the bus, tired and exhausted, looking around me at the faces of the people sitting around me. I knew them all, not personally, but for the past year, I had been seeing them every morning at the same time. I knew the curves on their faces and the style of their attire. I knew at what bus stop they would enter the bus and where they would get off. I also knew the miserable and tired look on their faces, a look that was screaming for change and greater meaning, as if the life they were living was one they never chose to live. I looked at them with pity, imagining their lives of working nine to five at dead-end jobs, living from pay check to pay check until they were old enough to retire, and I hoped they had good pension plans. That morning, I came to the realization that since I was also sitting on that bus every morning, I must have the same expression on my face.

I asked myself: What if this is life? What if what we were told as children about living our dreams and doing whatever we put our mind to, was completely false? Finally, I have awakened to this truth. Have I finally awakened to the truth?

As my mind was starting to wrap itself around that idea and that new way of thinking, I started to think about how I came to the world and about all the struggles my mother went through to have me. She frequently tells me stories of her working as a cleaning lady in a hotel and the difficulty of bending over to wash the big bath tubs while she was eight months pregnant. She tells me about how she took three buses and then the metro every time she had an appointment with her gynecologist during her pregnancy. She tells me her many stories of a young, poor immigrant woman, single, and pregnant with her first child, which was me. Then I also remembered an event from years ago that I'd completely forgotten about.

It was about the time when I was around eleven years old and I found in my mother's drawer a business card with my father's name on it. I am an only child, so to entertain myself, I would have to use my imagination and create different games that I could play on my own. One of my favorite games was playing detective and going through my mother's, grandmother's, and grandfather's things, hoping that I could find some kind of hidden treasure. I remember how much I enjoyed playing that game even though my mother would always ground me when she found out that I went through her things without her permission. My grandmother and grandfather would never say anything.

My father was a bicycle shop owner. On his business card there was the image of a bicycle, his full name, and the address and phone number of the shop. It was a white card with dark blue font on it, and even the image of the bicycle was printed in blue. On the back of the card, handwritten, was a phone number and on top, the name of a clinic. I took the card with me and for a few weeks, I didn't know whether I should or shouldn't tell my mother about what I had found in her drawer. When I finally found the courage to ask her if this really was my father's business card, she sat me down and told me the story.

My mother emigrated from Bolivia to Canada in her late twenties. She didn't know anybody, didn't speak English or French, and didn't have two pennies to rub together. She met my father and they started dating. After about a year, she found herself pregnant, and when she told my father, he told her that she needed to have an abortion because he wasn't ready to have children. He gave her the phone number of a clinic so that she could get an appointment to have the abortion procedure, and he wrote it down on the business card I found.

At that same time, my grandmother's immigration papers were finalized and she moved to Canada to come join my mother. My mother had already made the appointment at the clinic. Since she didn't have money, only spoke Spanish, didn't have a stable job, and now since she could clearly see that she wasn't going to have the support of my father, she felt like she had no other option. The day before the appointment, my grandmother found out that my mother was pregnant. She told my mother that if she were to proceed with the abortion, she was going back to Bolivia and she would never see my mother again. She was very serious. It was not a threat, it was a promise, and my mother could clearly see it. She ended up not keeping the appointment, and less than nine months later, I was born.

As I remembered this story on that morning, it was as if something lit up in me. It was as if all of a sudden I realized that it was true when our teachers told us that we can do whatever we put our minds to, that we can live our dreams. Actually, I thought, it is our responsibility to live our dreams. I realized that for all of that to happen to my mother and me, for all of the stars to align in that particular way at that particular time so that I would come to this world, was not just a coincidence. It was all designed divinely.

I know my mother now thinks of this in the same way that I do. She feels that all the struggles she went through and the sacrifices she made were nothing compared to how grateful she is to have her daughter.

Suddenly I knew I was meant for more—I was meant to do more. I rang the bell of the bus and got out at the next stop. I crossed the street and waited for the next bus to come and went back home. I called in sick that day and I did this for the next day, and the next day, and the next day. I stayed for weeks in my bedroom, reading and writing.

We all come into this world to different circumstances and have a different story about our arrival. Perhaps you were wanted and planned or maybe, like me, you were an accident or were what I like to call an unexpected surprise. Regardless of how you came to be, you are here for a reason, and the fact that all of the stars aligned in a way that allowed your parents to meet and to conceive you, goes to prove that your existence is not an accident of nature.

Think about it—what were the odds of you being here? What were the odds of your making it, out of the millions of sperms who traveled? You are the one who won the prize even though the chances of that happening were so small.

And if you take the time to study and analyze the nine months that a baby spends in their mother's womb, forming, growing, and becoming, you will be amazed at how miraculous the entire process is. You are a miracle, a reflection of God's infinite love and power. The same God that created the ocean, the mountains, the sky, and the animal kingdom has created you, and just like the ocean has its mission and purpose, you do too. Never doubt that.

One of the biggest mistakes people make in life is to settle on a career choice before they discover their personal mission. It's only when you know what your personal mission is that you will be able to choose a career that serves that mission. If you don't pursue a career that aligns with your purpose, in time you will end up feeling unfulfilled and unhappy. Teachers should learn to ask their young students not, "What do you want to do when you grow up?" but instead "What do you think is your purpose in life?"

You have to understand that what you do doesn't really matter; it's why you do it that matters. The why is what will make you wake up on Monday mornings when you are tired and didn't get enough sleep, the why is what will pull you through even when things at work are not going exactly how you'd like them to go. It's what makes some people whisper to themselves: "I love my job," while others are saying, "I can't wait to retire."

I know for sure that no matter what career I ended up with, I'd still want to be a vessel through which a message of love and inspiration would be carried to the world, because that's my personal mission, my purpose. Whether I had become a school teacher, a chef at a restaurant, or a clerk in a shop, I know that I would still be living within my purpose and using myself and my life to do what I came to planet Earth to do.

I believe that there are seven different categories of purposes. Before I explain each one of these categories, I want to clarify something. While I believe each and every one of us has a specific purpose, a mission that can only be accomplished by us, you will still have to figure out which personal mission within the category is the one you've been assigned. Time, experience, and intuition will help you to figure that out. For now, let's begin with the seven categories.

## 1. *To inspire*

You are the kind of person that people look up to for your strength, perseverance, and grace. You light up a room when you walk in, and when you open your mouth to tell your story or to try to motivate someone who is not feeling too well, everyone listens and soaks up your knowledge and wisdom. It is very possible that you've encountered many challenges throughout life, but it's those challenges that make you a remarkable person who has the ability to inspire others.

If your purpose is to inspire others, the kind of career that would fulfill you would be anything that puts you in contact with people, where you can speak to people and share your light with the world. Professions like politician, speaker, radio or television host, producer, and many others in the field of the arts, music, and communications would be a great fit for you.

## 2. *To protect*

Maybe you have younger brothers and sisters, and all your life you've played the role of the protector, or maybe you've always been the one standing up for your friends at school or for those who were bullied and mistreated. You have the ability and the desire to protect others, perhaps not only humans but also animals, our vegetation, and the planet. You have a very strong sense of compassion for any living being and all that Mother Nature has created.

If this description speaks to you, than you are a protector by nature, and the best kinds of professions for you are those in which you defend and protect. Police officer, military agent, animal activist, social worker, and other professions in the service field will fulfill you and your purpose.

## 3. *To heal*

You are a person who likes to make people feel good physically or emotionally. You take pleasure in relieving people's pain and suffering. Since you were a child, you were always the one putting a Band-Aid on your friend's "booboos" and always the one offering a massage to your mother and father after they had a long, stressful day at work. You are a healer at heart and healing others' deep pain is your calling.

Ideal professions for you would range from chiropractor and massage therapist to doctor and nurse, or perhaps to spiritual healer, a religious leader, or psychiatrist.

## 4. *To create*

You are always in the act of creating—whether it is artwork, do-it-yourself projects, writing, or inventing something. Your imagination is your greatest power and you use it to envision things before they come to fruition. Since you were a child, you could never stand still or simply play with the toys most kids loved, because you were always creating and inventing. You love crafts, projects, and ideas. They fire you up and passion rises in your heart when you do these things.

The perfect careers for you would be working as an inventor, architect, painter, writer, building constructor, or anything else that has to do with creating something whether it be physical or in the mind.

## 5. *To teach*

You are a teacher at heart. In everything that you do or say, you teach valuable lessons to the world. You feel most fulfilled when you get to share your knowledge with people, and every time that you learn something new, you teach it.

You have probably guessed that an ideal career in this field of purpose would be as a teacher but you can also become an author or an expert and lecturer in any field and still fulfill your life's mission.

## 6. *To help*

When someone is in need, you are always the first to help. Since you were a young child, you were always mommy's or daddy's little helper, people didn't even need to ask, because you were already there with your helping hat on. All careers in the service world are made for you.

This category of purpose has the most choices out of them all. The service world is so vast that everything that ranges from customer service, to first responders and medical personnel, to stewardess, to plumbers and electricians, can work for you.

## 7. *To nurture*

When friends come over, you always make sure that everyone is well fed and well hydrated. Always offering refills and asking repeatedly, "Are you hungry? I can make something to eat if you want." You are a nurturer and server. You also have a natural ability with babies and animals, you take care of them, give them love and affection, and spoil them with kisses. You are a nurturing being and you love to take care of people and make sure that everyone's stomach—and spirit—is full. A career in the culinary world would be a perfect fit for you. If not, you'd be great as a caregiver, a babysitter, or even as a nutritionist.

As you may have noticed, there are many times in life when you get to play in more than one category of purpose. The best example is by being a parent. When you become a parent, you get to explore all categories of purposes at once, which is why people unanimously agree on the fact that being a parent is the most fulfilling job and the most rewarding role a human can undertake. The problem with that, though, is that as the child grows up, the role of the parent changes and at some point, the child doesn't need you as their protector or nurturer or even as a helper, since he can make it on his own. This is when a lot of people find themselves empty. The "leaving the nest blues" is very common when people don't have a purpose of their own, when they made themselves believe that their personal mission was their children. But that's never possible because another human being can never be someone's personal mission or purpose.

## LET YOUR PURPOSE FIND YOU

People say that the two most important days of someone's life are the day they were born and the day they realize why they were born. You can spend years and years on this earth without knowing why you are here and living a life without purpose, but the day you find what it is that you can bring to this planet, meaning what your purpose is, that's when, I believe, you fully start living.

Les Brown once said, "When you are in alignment with why you are here, that gives you a sense of happiness and a sense of fulfillment and a sense of joy that passes all human understanding. Getting up in the morning and knowing the reason why you were chosen out of 400 million sperm to come here to do a work that is your assignment. To leave the world in better shape than how you found it. To bring something here that was not here before you showed up. When you know what that is and you go after that, that to me, is living life full and it gives you a sense of fulfillment that goes beyond who you are and has impact that unravels long after your box has been buried."

That is the best description of what is felt when you finally realize what your purpose in life is. There is no feeling that can compare. Think about the feeling you have when you're falling in love—the butterflies, the smile on your face whenever you think about that person, how it just seems like the air you breathe is purer and your sight is clearer; even the food you eat seems to taste better. Now imagine feeling that for yourself, for your life.

At this point, you may be asking yourself, "Alright, well how do I know in which category of purpose I fit and what my specific purpose is?" Truthfully, I have never seen someone find their purpose. However, what I have seen over and over again is purposes finding their vessels. See, all we really are in this world, are vessels through which we can express our highest calling, our grandest mission.

For your purpose to find you, one thing is for sure—you must be ready. You must be ready to receive it, to understand the magnitude and importance of it, and live by it. There are certain things that you can start doing today to prepare for the day of the revelation of your purpose.

*In preparation, spend more time alone.* Spending time alone with yourself as often as possible will allow you to quiet your mind and listen to the inner voice. The inner voice is there to guide you towards your divine destiny, which can only be fulfilled through a life of purpose.

*Study, read, and learn.* Be open to new ideas, philosophies, and to learning. Studying is the path to enlightenment, so study. One of the biggest issues that we have today in our society is that the educational system teaches a very narrow way of thinking to our youth and only puts emphasis on certain topics and ignores others. Mathematics, science, and English are indeed very important topics, but what about self-love, multi-religious theology, and relationships? Aren't they equally as important, or perhaps a little more important, than what we are taught in most public schools across America? They say that knowledge is power and lack of knowledge is lack of power, so the more you learn, the more you open your mind, the more you are likely to attract your purpose to you. Purposes only find those who are enlightened.

*Open your mind and spirit.* Your purpose will never find you if you are not willing to receive it. If you are close-minded when it comes to the topic of life purposes, and you don't believe that you have a mission for this lifetime, your purpose will never come to you. Why would it? So that you can ignore it or never live by it? If you are too busy neglecting its existence, your purpose will neglect you. Remember that whatever you believe to be true is true. If you believe that you don't have a purpose for this lifetime, you don't. If you believe you have a purpose for this lifetime, you do, and it's coming to you.

*Be at peace.* A state of peace, bliss, and joy is needed for your purpose to walk into your life. Your purpose can't find you if you have clutter, needless drama, and grey clouds following you around. You need to first let go of all the negativity in order to allow clarity for your mission to find its way to you. Fill yourself up with positivity and, most importantly, love, which is the main purpose of the human species. Not your individual mission but your collective one.

## THE COLLECTIVE MISSION

Not only do we have a specific mission assigned to each and every one of us, but we also have a collective mission—a mission we all share and we all live for. This purpose is what maintains the levels of goodness and beauty in the world, a lack of this can bring our species to extinction and destruction. Our collective purpose is to love—to love life, others, and ourselves. Love is the highest form of energy in the world, and when we vibrate and live in love, positivity, beauty, and even life, are created.

⌒⌒⌒

I have yet to learn the secrets of life, or perhaps I have them all hidden inside of me. All I know is that we are all being used for something greater than ourselves, and everyone that we meet and every situation that we encounter brings us closer to that moment of sharing and giving. The moment when we are completely selfless we will understand that our lives are simple instruments for the evolution of love and peace for future generations. As we grow, physically at first, then mentally, and spiritually at last, we finally can open our three eyes and see that beyond our small lives and everything we can see and touch, there lies the importance of our existence and the power of our time here on planet Earth.

I wish more people could understand this truth and realize that it is not about them; it never has been. We often get so caught up in our lives and our day-to-day existence that we become selfish. Yet we don't think we are because we care about those around us—our family, friends, kids, parents, husband or wife—but even then, the selfishness prevails. We don't realize that our small world around us needs our love, time, and attention, but the world outside of us, needs us even more. You can love and you can care for those who surround you, but you must not forget or neglect the extended family of humanity that you have yet to meet and love.

Long ago, I realized that this human experience is not about me; it is about something greater than I could ever even hope to be. The knowing of that makes every decision that I make wiser. And I know for sure that it will do the same thing for you.

# 10
# Women's Work

*Men may work from sun to sun but women's work is never done.*

—A WELL-KNOWN ADAGE

## WE CAN DO IT

Throughout history, women have shown their strength over and over again. Mary, mother of Jesus, watched her son die on the cross; Joan of Arc fought for an entire country; Mother Teresa devoted her life to the service of the poor; and so many other great women showed and proved to us that yes, we can do it.

The following is a well-known saying: "Whether you think you can or whether you think you can't, you are right." As women, we have been conditioned to believe that we can't have it all and we can't do it all. However, we have proved the world wrong on many occasions. The work that you have to do on Earth has already chosen you; all you have to do is receive it with wide-open arms. Perhaps you already know what it is. If you don't, continue being open and it will come to you before you finish reading this book. In this chapter I call it *the work*, but in previous chapters in the book, I have called it your purpose or your mission.

If you already know what the work is that you have been brought to this world to do, you have probably already started to create your vision—the grand vision. This is the image you create in your mind of what it will look like, what it will feel like, and what you will hear the moment that this dream comes to pass. I will dive into this in a few moments. After creating the vision, you will have to create the master plan. Few people come up with a master plan and therefore fail. It is often said that failing to plan is like planning to fail.

The greatest people who have changed the world before us, both men and women, knew very well what their grand vision and the master plan were, whether or not that was what they named it. I see this as being a triangle. At the point on the top, we have the Mission, which is your purpose, or your work to be accomplished. On the left corner at the base of the triangle of the pyramid there is the Vision, and in the opposite corner at the base of the triangle is the Strategy, which is the plan. Whoever wishes to succeed needs to pay close attention to this triangle and know what each entails. Without the connection of a Mission, a Vision, and Strategy, no work or mission can be completed.

In the chapter "Purposeful Living," I have explained what the mission is all about and how you can discover it. In this chapter, I will explain what the vision and the strategy are and how to use them to do the work that you have been chosen to do.

Women's work is more important than ever before. You have been chosen to accomplish a specific mission on this earth and being Beyond Beauty is about not ignoring this calling, it's about living a life of purpose and contribution. To do so, you must first understand how to do the work.

## THE GRAND VISION

The grand vision is the vision and image of what will be when all is said and done, when dreams are no longer dreams and have become a reality.

Without a vision, you will get nowhere. It is simply impossible; it's like trying to make a puzzle in the dark; if you don't have vision, you can't put the pieces where they're supposed to be in order to complete the great puzzle. Your dream, your work, your goal, your mission—however you want to refer to it—is the puzzle to be solved, and you need the vision to do this.

I want you to envision what it will be like ten, twenty, thirty, and even ninety years from now. Long after you will have left planet Earth, what will your legacy be? What will you have left behind?

When I first began to make extreme changes in my life and realize what the work was that I wanted to do in the world, one of the first things that I took the time to create was a vision board. I had heard so many positive comments and success stories about people who used the vision board in their lives to attract whatever it was that they wanted. I simply had to try it just to see if it was going to work for me.

I remember I took a big wooden board that I painted black, a bunch of magazines, a pair of scissors and some glue, and I began building my own personalized vision board. On that vision board was a concrete image of everything that I wanted to have, and showed myself in places where I wanted to be, and images of things that I wanted to accomplish within the next six to twelve months.

I hung the big board in my bedroom so that I could see it every single day. I remember when I was cutting the images, I found one of a clock. On the top it read, "Will Return." Back then, I was recovering from a bad ending to a relationship, and I wanted the man who broke my heart to come back into my life for pride and egoistic reasons. So I put that little image of a clock on the board, with no one other than me knowing what it really meant. After a few months, I was staring at the vision board realizing how every image had somehow manifested itself into my life. I took a look at the clock and the arrows were pointing at the numbers 1 and 6. I thought to myself, how ironic would it be if these numbers would represent the day and month of when he "will return." Truthfully I didn't care anymore since the feelings were long gone. I had moved on but that thought stayed in my mind.

A few days before the beginning of June, we bumped into each other. He spent the first few weeks of June pursuing me without success. You can say that it was a coincidence if you want, but before you say that, I recommend that you create a vision board and see for yourself.

There is a reason why God brought us all here. We have a work assigned to us all and I want you to start living by your passion. Look around you, look at what people are doing, and look at all the ordinary people who are surrounded by ordinary friends and who are living an ordinary life. Use them as an example of what you don't want to be. Stop setting limits for yourself, because you are the only one who can do that; no one else can do that for you. Whatever goal you have in mind, know that you are able to achieve it. And always remember that a dream would not have been created inside of you if you didn't have the capacity to achieve it.

If there is one thing that I have learned from life, it is that when you put a desire or a thought out in the universe, that thought or desire will find its way into your life. I believe that this is what makes life worth living. One of the most magnificent miracles of life is the fact that we can imagine something in our mind and want it so badly that all the stars align in our favor so that we finally get it.

## THE MASTER PLAN

I remember how back in high school teachers would ask us what it was that we wanted to do later on in our life, and as soon as we answered, they asked if there were anything else we wanted to do, a backup plan, a Plan B.

For many years I used to have various backup plans. At first, probably until the age of eleven, I wanted to be a singer. The world around me kept telling me that the chances to make it in that field were slim. So I got discouraged and changed my mind. Afterwards, I decided I wanted to be an architect, but since I wasn't a good illustrator, I dropped that plan. Then I thought I could be a good lawyer, but since I didn't enjoy school and the way the educational system is set up, and I couldn't see myself spending years in law school, I put that plan to the side as well. Then it was an interior designer, then real estate agent, then teacher, and the list goes on.

As time and the years were passing by, my plans were always changing and none of them were working. As soon as something was not going the right way, I would give up and jump to Plan B or C or D or . . . Well, you get the picture right? I did the whole alphabet and finally stopped the merry-go-round and asked myself why it was that my first plan didn't work out.

Coming up with a plan is something that anyone can do. Having a plan is easy; the hard part is making it happen. I believe that turning your plan into a master plan is the key to success. There are five fundamental steps that anyone who wants to accomplish their goal, mission, work, dream, purpose, no matter what it is, has to go through in order to be successful. Here they are:

***Define Your Goal:*** Too many times, too many people make the same mistake. They have a backup plan when in reality having a backup plan is something absolutely useless and only there to distract you from your Plan A. If you have a lifelong dream, how can you replace it with a backup dream? How can someone say, "Okay, well if I don't become an actor, I can always be a plumber?" A bitter plumber, you should say. Never allow yourself to settle for less than your heart's true desire.

The first step is really to define what your dream is and stick to it, to know what it is that you want to accomplish no matter how big that goal is. Once you find what that goal is, write it down on a piece of paper that you will see and read every day. That's very important!

The second thing you have to write on that paper is when you will know that you have achieved your goal. For example, if your goal is to be a singer, will you feel like your goal has been attained after you release your first album or is it going to be after you sell a million copies of that album? It could also be after you win your first award or when you can purchase a certain car you always wanted to have. You have to define what success is to you because it varies depending on the person.

People who are successful are those who make decisions and don't change their decisions. People who are indecisive or who make a decision and always change it cannot succeed.

***Create Your Plan of Action:*** To make your dreams come true, you have to have a plan because yes, it's nice to know what your dreams are, but if you just sit around and wait for things to happen, you will be sitting around for a long time. I can guarantee you that. Every business writes a business plan before launching their services or products, and you have to make one too. You can't just sit around watching television and wishing that everything will simply work its way out and that God will come serve you your dreams on a golden platter. A plan is the heart of your goal; it's like the motor of a car. If there is no motor, no matter how beautiful the car looks and how great and fast it has the potential to be, without the motor the car will go nowhere. List the specific steps you have to take to attain that ultimate goal of yours. Be very precise, and use tools such as planners, agendas, and project sheets to help you organize your steps towards your dream life.

***Work Step-by-Step:*** Patience is also very important. You can't rush things and think that everything is going to be easy and that in the blink of an eye your goal will be accomplished. Read the story of any great man or woman in history who has accomplished something incredible and see how much time it took them and how they took step-by-step actions towards the accomplishment of their dream.

The steps are part of your plan. Every step should come with a deadline, because if you don't set a timeline for yourself, procrastination will eventually kill your dreams.

***Control Your Thoughts:*** Controlling your thoughts is difficult to do when most of the time the people around you will tell you how impossible and out of reach your dream is. That's when the chapter Free Feminine is important. You can't have an entourage of people who are negative because they will unconsciously destroy your dreams. You have to think positively and believe in yourself and in your capacity to make anything you want become reality.

How many hours does Oprah have in a day? The answer is twenty-four. How many hours do you have in a day? Once again the answer is twenty-four. Therefore why can someone like Oprah, who started from the bottom with empty pockets, succeed and become one of the greatest women today and you can't? There is no excuse, not your background, your education, your financial status—nothing is a good excuse to prevent the world from receiving your gifts, talents, and great work.

***Stop at Nothing:*** Failure is usually only temporary. People always say that after the rain comes the sun, right? That means that after every failure can come a great success. A major mistake that most people do is to give up right after the first small sign of failure. You can't think that everything will work your way and there will be no bumps along the road, because I can guarantee you that there will be many disappointments on the road to making your dreams become reality. If you have the engine, the transmission system, the body of the vehicle and the speed all combined, it is not an empty tank that can stop you. Once it gets empty, fill it back up and don't worry about the bumps on the road. There are way too many people in the world who unfortunately give up on their goals because of small setbacks. They don't realize that that is like having one flat tire and deciding to slash the other three.

Those were the five steps, or shall I say the five rules, to making your dreams and goals come true. Of course it's not an easy process. Truth be told, it is very hard, but in the end it will be worth the time and the sacrifices.

I like to believe that life is a big mountain, similar to Mount Everest. At the beginning of our journey, we are all standing at the bottom of the mountain. The bottom, of course, is always crowded. You hear people saying how they tried climbing the mountain and failed, and you hear others say how they hurt themselves trying to climb, and everyone around you is mostly complaining and saying how impossible it is to make it to the top. Yet when you look up, you see a small number of people standing at the top of that mountain, so you think to yourself, well if some people made it to the top, maybe I can make it as well. When you tell everyone else about your desire to climb the mountain, they all warn you and tell you that you shouldn't try because the chances of making it all the way to the top are slight.

That's the moment in your life when you have to make a choice—you can either listen to the people standing at the bottom who say that it's impossible to make it to the top, or you can ignore them all, knowing that it is possible because people before you made it. If you decide to not even try to climb that mountain, you lose; it's as simple as that. You stay at the bottom with all your fellow losers.

But if you decide to start climbing, you first have to know that it's going to be hard, you are possibly going to hurt yourself, and you are most likely going to fall at some point and have to get yourself up and perhaps start all over again. There will be days when you are going to be fed up, and the top of that mountain is going to seem to be so far away that you want to just stop climbing and stay where you are.

Many people have the nerve to start climbing, but they give up in the middle of the climb to the top because they've learned how to settle for less. They get comfortable and complacent. Yes, they are not at the bottom, but they are not at the top either. They just stay in the middle with all the average people who had dreams and hopes of making it to the summit but gave up. Persistence in life is so important because once you make it to the top, it will be worth all the effort.

Since on your way to the top there will be failure and disappointments, it will be your choice to either give up or make it. The people at the bottom of the mountain will start criticizing you, saying that you are selfish and that you changed because you left them all at the bottom. Or they might claim that you are not going to make it, and it's just a matter of time before you come back down. At the beginning when you start climbing, you're still going to hear them and their negative comments will affect you and make you doubt yourself. But as you go higher and higher the voices will start to fade away.

Many people are afraid to aim for the top because if they do, and fall back down, they fear what people may say or think; they fear the humiliation of trying and failing tremendously. That's the ego that cares about what people think. The heart, however, just follows its intuition and true calling.

Here's a quotation I love on this topic. It's an excerpt from the speech *Citizenship in a Republic*.

It is not the critic who counts; not the man who points out how the strong man stumbles, or where the doer of deeds could have done them better. The credit belongs to the man who is actually in the arena, whose face is marred by dust and sweat and blood; who strives valiantly; who errs, who comes short again and again, because there is no effort without error and shortcoming; but who does actually strive to do the deeds; who knows great enthusiasms, the great devotions; who spends himself in a worthy cause; who at the best knows in the end the triumph of high achievement, and who at the worst, if he fails, at least fails while daring greatly, so that his place shall never be with those cold and timid souls who neither know victory nor defeat.

—THEODORE ROOSEVELT
Speech delivered at the Sorbonne, Paris, France,
April 23, 1910

## AND MIRACLES . . .

Have you ever had one of those days when everything goes wrong? When I say everything, I mean literally everything. Your alarm doesn't ring in the morning and then when you're running late for work it starts to rain, the heel on your stiletto breaks, your boss is mad at you, and it just keeps on coming—one bad event after another bad event, and you just keep repeating to yourself, "This is not my day!"

The universe is just like the genie in the movie *Aladdin*, but the universe is much more generous than he was. You are granted many more than three wishes; as a matter of fact, you get as many wishes as you want, believe it or not. So whenever you say, "This is not my day," your personal genie responds by saying, "Your wish is my command!"

The way you feel is the way your life will go. Feel negative, and you will bring more negativity. Cry and you will bring more reasons to cry. You have to be very careful with the words you use to be aware whether they are negative or positive. Ultimately, you are the person whom you listen to the most, and whatever you say affects your life. That's just the way it goes, so it's time to start thinking before you wish for something because you just might get what you wish for!

A few events happened in my life that made me discover there is something out there, a force extremely powerful that can't be explained, yet it exists. Before I began to study the law of attraction, I learned by experience that you really can get what you want, regardless of what it is. If you believe that you can't, well guess what, you can't. But if you are convinced that you can, well you can.

On January 1, 2008, the year that I moved out of my parent's house, months before I even knew that I was going to move, I wrote on a small piece of paper what I wanted to accomplish during that year. I do the same thing every January 1st. I write on a small piece of paper what I want to achieve for the year to come. I hide it so that for the next 365 days I don't see it, and on the eve of the next new year, I unfold the little paper and see if I have accomplished what I set out to achieve 365 days before this. I began that little ritual at the beginning of my teenage years, and every single year I am amazed to see that somehow I always achieve the goal on the paper.

I will always remember at the end of that year that I moved out of my parent's house, when I was in my new apartment and celebrating New Year's Eve with all my friends and with the man that I was in love with. It was a beautiful night with champagne, great food, New Year's decorations everywhere, and everyone was so happy and having a great time. A few minutes before midnight, I went into my bedroom alone to look for the little note I had written on January 1st of that year. I unfolded it and on it was written, "I just want to live the good life." The ten-second countdown began, I went in the living room to join everyone and there it was on my living room wall, "Welcome to the good life." That was the kind of moment that you know you will never forget—the good feelings, the noise of celebration, the confetti everywhere, and the smiles on everyone's face, but most importantly the sudden realization that you can have whatever you want in life.

When my friend and I moved into that apartment, one of the first things that we did was to write on the main bright red wall of our living room that message of "Welcome to the good life." At that time we were both young and that's all we really wanted. The day we wrote that, I had no memory whatsoever that eight months earlier I had written on a little piece of paper that I just wanted to live the good life. As a matter of fact, eight months earlier, at the beginning of 2008, I had no plans at all to move out of my parent's house. I remember when I wrote about wanting to live the good life on that little piece of paper, I had no idea how I was going to make that happen, when I was still living at my mother's house, had no plans for my future and didn't have much money.

Of course today, my definition of living a good life is much different than what it was when I was eighteen years old, but at the time, the good life for me and for most people of my age, was to be able to go out and party almost every night, have nice luxurious things, dress nicely, have money, and all of the other superficialities that the media sells to the youth. All those things were part of my reality when eight months earlier they were nothing but a wish.

The law of attraction, which I like to call "The Miracle," as it was called for centuries, says you have a desire, you pray for it, and then suddenly you have it—your wish becomes a reality. The law of attraction is as real as the law of gravity; there is not really a way to explain how and why it operates the way it does, but we know that it is there and has been there since the beginning of time. The Bible states clearly: Ask and you shall receive.

We are subject to negativity everywhere we go—in the newspapers, on the television, and everywhere we turn. We are most likely to see on the front page of a newspaper an article about someone who was murdered, but of course you will never see a news article about a woman who just gave birth to a beautiful healthy baby. We are bombarded by all the negative events that are occurring on Earth, so at the end of the day, our mind is easily filled with negativity.

Therefore, you must learn how to guard your mind and thoughts. Turn off the television, close the newspaper, and when someone starts speaking negatively about another person, leave the room. Every day you have the choice to either have a good or a bad day. It is really up to you. Make sure you use this universal law, called the law of attraction, to your benefit by always attempting to see the positive side of things, by always choosing, if possible, to feel love-based emotions, by always focusing on your work and purpose, by always trying to surround yourself with beauty and grace.

The people who get to live for their passion and make their dreams come true have faith. They embrace their dreams and know that they are possible and are not too good to be true. You have to ignore that inner doubting voice in your subconscious mind and stop listening to the negative people who surround you and who are constantly telling you that your goal is out of reach.

In chapter 8, I talked about becoming a queen. A queen is never afraid of failure. She looks at it dead in the eye and repeats the same words that Joan of Arc once said with the same strength, courage, and conviction, "I am not afraid, I was born to do this."

I'd finish this chapter by sharing with you a truly inspiring quote from the President of the United States of America:

> Making your mark on this world is hard. If it were easy, everybody would do it. But it's not. It takes patience, it takes commitment, and it comes with plenty of failure along the way. The real test is not whether you avoid this failure because you won't. It's whether you let it harden you or shame you into inaction or whether you learn from it, whether you choose to persevere.
>
> —BARACK OBAMA
> Northwestern University Commencement Address
> June 16, 2006

# 11

# *The Feminine Power*

*The repression of the feminine has led to a planet on the edge of collapse.*
*The re-emergence is going to be a dance to behold.*
—CLARE DAKIN, *Founder of Tree Sisters*

## REDEFINING FEMALE EMPOWERMENT

When we hear the term female empowerment, we think of women burning their bras in public. We think of groups of feminists bashing men and blaming them for everything that is wrong in the world today. We think of the iconic We Can Do It photograph of Geraldine Hoff wearing a polka-dotted bandana on her head and showing her muscles, portraying more masculinity than anything else.

Even when you Google female empowerment, you will often see images of masculine-oriented figures and representations of men. Along with images of women degrading men are quotations from women saying things like "We are not Queens, but Kings." It seems as if the female empowerment of today should be called masculine re-empowerment because everything that we do and say when it comes to empowering women ends up being a re-empowerment of the masculine energy in the world. We seem to be so caught up trying to constantly be men or be like men that we have forgotten about the beautiful feminine essence. At times, I feel like women are ashamed to be women, and that if we had the choice, we would choose to be men. But this has got to change.

For centuries, we have been conditioned to believe that whatever men do is always better, more exciting, and more important than what women do. We have been told that nurturing and raising our children is less important than going out in the world to make money and provide material things for the family. Slowly, we have grown with the yearning of wanting to resemble daddy and be less like mommy.

There is nothing wrong in wanting to have a career and to make your own money. To the contrary, I strongly encourage this for women. It allows us to be free and feel a sense of security. The right to work is a wonderful thing. The problem starts the moment we begin to believe that a woman who works in the corporate world is more important than a woman who is a stay-at-home mom. It starts the moment we focus our energy on envying men instead of focusing it on ourselves

Most men have never needed to envy the role of women because they have traditionally been in positions of power and were never taught to be discontent with their own roles. They have never complained about the fact that we can wear skirts, which are often more comfortable and freeing than pants, and they can't. They never bemoaned the fact that we are the ones who breastfeed the children and they can't. They rarely protest about the fact that nature chose us to carry a child in our womb and they don't have that gift. Most men are in no way, shape, or form envious of the rights, abilities, or roles that we, as women, have. Unlike us, they are proud and content with their own roles, because those roles were never demeaned.

Female empowerment often becomes all about trying to put the opposite sex down and pointing the finger at them when it comes to faults and wrongdoings. We've been wrong all along. Female empowerment isn't about disempowering the opposite sex, rather it is about empowering our femininity and our womanhood. Female empowerment should be all about helping one another, as females, to be the best women that we can be and not be ashamed of our roles and our essence. Obviously men and women are very different in many ways. Men and women have different abilities and powers, and what we need to do is to own ours instead of trying to steal and appropriate the ones that men have.

Female empowerment needs to be redefined; it needs to become what it was always supposed to be—an empowerment of the feminine energy and of the Goddess within. The time has come for us to awaken to this and to cease putting so much emphasis on masculine energy, which the world is already so full of, and instead promote the feminine energy.

Masculine and feminine energy are both necessary in this world, but at this present moment in time, there is a major imbalance between the energies. Men and women tend to worship the masculine and dismiss the feminine, causing a deficit of feminine energy in the universe and creating a lot of chaos and dysfunction.

## THE DIVINE MASCULINE AND THE DIVINE FEMININE

The masculine and the feminine are both divine. Both of these energies are flowing in your spirit, whether you are a man or a woman. These are the yin and the yang, the God and the Goddess. The major imbalance of energies in the world at this present time has been existent for centuries now. Women and men have been resisting the divine feminine for way too long. We have not only resisted it, we have been repulsed and ashamed by it.

We've been taught that being feminine is weak and that it is only by being masculine that we can succeed in life. Perhaps we haven't been told these things directly and verbally, but it has been shown to us over and over again. Expressions and ideas such as "You run like a girl," "Be a man, man up!" or "Grow some balls," all insinuate that being masculine is better than being feminine.

In the seventies, American women stood up for past generations and all generations of women to come. They fought for our rights and have achieved a great deal for us all. Because of their fight, we are now able to work in the same fields as men and feel we have greater rights to pursue the careers that men traditionally had. The problem is that most by-products of the seventies have been in resistance to their own divine feminine without knowing it. Most feminists are in actuality "masculists," as I like to call them, under the guise that they are for empowerment of the feminine. What we all must understand is that rising to power for women has nothing to do with decreasing the power of men. We must stop trying to resemble men and have what men have, and start expressing our femininity instead of suppressing it.

Masculine and feminine energy are both very different and have distinct aspects that represent each one of them. As we embark in this new Age of Aquarius, there is a major shift in the energies of the universe and there seems to be a reemergence of the divine feminine. However, this does not mean that we shall forget about the divine masculine. The balance which will be restored in the Age of Aquarius is about both energies rising into power.

We may live in a patriarchal society, but this does not mean that the divine masculine is in power. Masculinity should not be associated with being a jerk, which in today's society it is. The masculine power is just as divine as the feminine but men and women are associating it with false and demeaning interpretations of masculinity. When you think of masculinity perhaps you think of a college jock or a macho, but this is not the divine masculine, it is a pretense of it.

## Aspects of the Divine Masculine

The aspects of the divine masculine are fatherhood, growth, transformation, action, protection, direction, movement, responsibility, strength, focus, clarity, intellect, authority, generosity, abundance, and encouragement, and in many cultures there is a male god of the sun.

The divine masculine is represented by the God, the King, the Warrior, the Sage, and the Passionate Lover.

As I said, we may live in a patriarchal society, but the divine masculine is not in power. The protector and the warrior is not well represented today. This is a shame. We have men and women who pretend to be masculine and strong, yet on the inside are weak and frail. They use competition, domination, and control to gain power and rule the world, which is why this world is in such a terrible and deteriorating state.

To create more genuine divine masculine energy in the world today, we must first take a look at our relationship with our father. The first interaction we had with the masculine was with our father. Therefore, the thoughts and feelings that we hold toward him determine our relationship with the divine masculine.

In order to create more masculine energy in the universe, men and even women can begin by taking responsibility, which is one of the aspects of the divine masculine. Taking responsibility, being decisive, and taking initiative helps create masculine energy. As a matter of fact, everything that has to do with taking action, such as initiation and engaging in the pursuit of a job opportunity, or in approaching a woman to ask her out on a date, is masculine.

Momentum and forward motion help manifest more masculine energy as well. And finally, growing and developing new skills and therefore creating more confidence definitely will unleash the masculine power.

## *Aspects of the Divine Feminine*

The aspects of the divine feminine are nurturing, sensuality, harmony, connection, wisdom, intuition, openness, creation, love, birth, healing, motherhood, forgiveness, insight, receptivity, restoration, life, renewal, understanding, compassion, beauty, and in many cultures the female is the moon goddess.

The divine feminine is represented by the Goddess, the Queen, the Priestess, the Sweet Lover, and the Wise Woman.

To awaken the Queen within you, you have to first examine your resistance to the divine feminine. Examine it, understand where it comes from, and heal it. Most of our resistance comes from our mothers, since our first introduction to the divine feminine is our relationship with our mother. To heal this resistance, remember the ideas that she transmitted to you. Perhaps she told you that you should be strong and not show emotion and be very logical and radical, which conflicts with the divine feminine essence. The feminine is all about intuition and emotion, so if you were raised by a mother who never allowed you to develop those aspects, you are suffering today, as your feminine essence cannot flourish.

First, understand that your mother only taught you what she thought she knew was right. Maya Angelou said, "When you know better, you do better." Now that you know better, you must do better. It doesn't happen overnight, but start today to be comfortable with showing emotion and being in tune with your intuition. Don't be ashamed of it, as you have been taught to be. Be proud of the Goddess that you are.

Another great way to awaken the divine feminine is through the act of creating. Feminine essence is all about creation, which is why we create life. To do this, you can use art, dance, music, or other forms of creation. This will help you to be in touch with your divine feminine and the Goddess within.

Collaborate and cultivate openness and compassion and love. Opening up to the world and collaborating with others, especially with other women, helps your femininity flow and blossom.

And finally, another way to unleash your feminine power is by exploring beauty and sensuality. Your body is a beautiful temple and you should not be ashamed of it. This doesn't mean that you should carelessly parade your sacred body to the world, but you should definitely explore it with your partner or even on your own. Make sure that your surroundings reflect beauty and sensuality. Flowers around the house, bubble baths, beautiful art pieces, and the use of vivid colors will help your feminine side awaken.

As women, we have been taught to be ashamed of our feminine side. We are often portrayed as being weak, confused, and emotionally unstable beings. It is popularly said that women are complicated and that our emotions are like roller coasters. How many times have you heard men say to you or to another woman, "I guess she's having her period!" or "Are you PMS-ing?" Our womanhood has become a mockery to the world and as a result, we have distanced ourselves from it.

## WHY MANY WOMEN HAVE BECOME MASCULINIZED

I have elaborated earlier about the different aspects of the divine masculine and the divine feminine. Out of all those aspects, the four primary ones are nurturing, receiving, doing, and giving. These traits are present in all of us but some less than others. As generation Y women, we have trouble with the nurturing and receiving aspects, especially in our relationships with the opposite sex.

More and more children are being raised in single-parent homes, and they often grow up with the belief that one should never depend on anyone because the parental relationship did not work out. This is a significant source of the independent woman mentality that young women have today. Millennial women frequently refuse in any way, shape, or form to be dependent on a man. It can be a good thing at times; however, it can also cause friction and dysfunction in relationships. Women aren't allowing themselves to receive any more because they unconsciously fear that if they receive something from a man, it will make them dependent on him, which is not the case. Young women don't let the man pay on the first date, or open the door, or pull out a chair for them.

As women, we don't allow men to take the initiative anymore, and then we complain about how men of this generation don't know how to be gentlemen. It's because we are not allowing them to be. Most of the time, our masculine energy is so potent and our feminine energy so minimal that the opposite sex is forced to dim their masculine energy in our presence.

All of this began happening as a result to the feminist movement of the seventies. Without knowing it or realizing it, we fear that things might go back to how they were before, and because of this we build up walls and try to be as masculine as possible. Because we fear losing our rights and equality, we endlessly try to be as equal as possible to men, and therefore we try to embody the masculine energy as much as we can, not realizing that we all need to have a balance within us.

We see it all the time, strong, smart, independent . . . and single women. These women have rejected and excluded every single aspect of the feminine, more particularly the two most important ones of nurturing and receiving. They are so caught up in the masculine world, constantly giving and doing, that they completely unlearned how to allow themselves to be more feminine. And their romantic relationships are paying the price.

In order for you to fully understand the importance of maintaining a balance between the two energies, masculine and feminine, let me illustrate an example for you.

You wake up in the morning, make yourself a cup of tea, and you spend about half an hour contemplating what you are going to do and accomplish during the day. Contemplation is generated by the feminine energy. During your contemplative time you think about the things that you want to change or create, which is part of the feminine energy. When you are done visualizing your day in your mind, you finally get up and you pick up the phone to make a few calls, perhaps to contact potential clients. Getting up and making the call, therefore doing, is part of the masculine energy. You are taking action, which puts the masculine energy to work. Later on, you feel the need to take a walk and get some fresh air. As you are walking around your neighborhood, you begin to run through your mind your actions for the rest of the day, using once again your creativity and visualizing aspects. And finally as the day evolves, you continue to take action and bring to fruition what you had envisioned.

This example shows how the masculine and feminine energy both cooperate with one another. They are both necessary, and without connecting the creative force that is the feminine essence with the action-driven powers of the masculine essence, nothing can be born. It is synonymous to a child being born. Without the center of creation that lies within the womb of the woman and the power of the masculine-giving energy, there can be no conception of a child. The woman receives and the man gives. It is the way nature intended us to be—it's the way conception happens, whether it be of a child, or of a goal.

As women of generation Y, we must fearlessly regain our feminine essence. That way we will be able to work harmoniously and in balance with the masculine energy. Accepting the feminine aspects within ourselves will help us bring back more balance within the world.

## FEMINISM FOR REAL

The same way I want to redefine female empowerment, I also want to redefine feminism. Feminism has to fully and truly embrace femininity. All women must learn how to be proud of their feminine essence in order to restore the divine feminine principles and bring the Goddess back.

Most women of today are not conscious of their feminine values and have lost themselves in trying to be superior to men. It is no longer about equality; women of today seem to want it all, especially all that men have. We have so much anger and resentment toward the masculine power of the world that we think that the only way is to become more powerful than men in order to make us superior to them, but this is not the right way to do things. Feminism should be about the divine feminine and our ability to be intuitive, emotional, loving, and caring. We have to learn how to be proud of our gifts.

Men are from Mars and women are from Venus, they say. We are distinct from one another and there is nothing wrong with that. We are the caring aspect and men are the aspect of force, if we renounce our role in this universe, humanity will not find salvation.

Very often, when I speak about this topic, I get a lot of flak from the "masculists" who like to call themselves feminists. Their response is, "Why are men the force of action and not women," and this is where the problem begins. Why wouldn't you want to be the aspect of caring and nurturing? Why do you feel in your mind that force is better than care? It's the unconscious programming that you have been subject to. You have been told over and over again that whatever is masculine is better than what is feminine. I can already hear some women say, "Well that's the point: why is force masculine and not feminine?" We have turned into the jealous and envious ugly stepsister, always wanting what the other has. But as we are so caught up trying to have what men have, we forget what a blessing it is to be divinely feminine.

In order to achieve a real age of female empowerment and honest feminism, we have to stand together in alliance. Patriarchy will continue to rule as long as women continue to hate and compete with one another. The key to fully entering the Age of Aquarius is cooperation and solidarity among women and men. Women, let's set the example!

We, as women, give inspiration to the world, and mostly to men. The woman looks after the man as the man supports the woman. If the man is earth, the woman is water. They can both coexist and are equally as important to the survival of humanity. For this world to find balance again, it is our responsibility to create more love. If we continue to neglect our feminine energy, this world will never find peace. However, if we at last embrace our feminine energy and become real feminists, a major positive shift will be on its way.

Yes, misogyny still exists, and despite the recent social and political emancipation in many countries around the world, women are still subject to oppression, sexism, and injustice. We have come a long way but we still have much road to travel. Women in the seventies have fought fearlessly for us, and thanks to them we have accomplished a great deal. It is now up to us, Generation Y, to continue the work, but instead of fighting with aggression, violence, and warlike ideologies, let's use love, compassion, and the feminine energy.

The mistake that was made during the feminist movement was that women fought for their rights, but at the same time gave up their enjoyment and appreciation of the values of being feminine. It's as if women thought that they couldn't have it all. They felt that if they gained the right to have the same benefits as men in our work and the rights of being socially equal to men, they would have to give up on their femininity. Most women today have female bodies but masculine minds. We can now work, but we don't know how to care for our children and men. We can now have power, but we can't cry or show other feelings because we don't want to be seen as too emotional. We can now have a say in things at home and in our community, but we can't show our intuitive powers in fear of being judged.

We have given up on what makes us women, on what brings the yin that the world is right now longing for. Generation Y, I call upon you to bring the Feminine Power back.

# 12

# The Gift of Beauty

*Beauty is a great gift of heaven; not for the purpose of female vanity,*
*but a great gift for one who loves, and wishes to be beloved.*

—MARIA EDGEWORTH
Nineteenth century Anglo-Irish novelist

## THE MOST BEAUTIFUL WOMAN
## IN THE ROOM

I remember watching an interview many years ago with a retired super model who back in the eighties was known to be the sexiest, prettiest, one of the most beautiful woman in the fashion industry. I can clearly remember what she said during that interview. When asked the question, "How was it to be the most beautiful woman in the room everywhere you went?" she replied, and I am paraphrasing, "I was never the most beautiful woman in the room; however, I was always the most confident one. During every photo shoot and during every fashion and runway event, before walking into the room, the stage, or the set, I would repeat to myself, I am the most beautiful, sexy, and smart woman here, over and over again, even if I knew it was not true. There was always a more beautiful, a sexier, and a smarter person everywhere I went, but I would enter every space believing that I was *it*."

The interviewer went on to say that was the powerful energy she successfully projected. Every time she walked into a room, all heads would turn and men would fall to their knees, not because that ex-super-model was the most beautiful, but simply because she was the most confident.

Throughout this book, I put a lot of emphasis on self-confidence and self-esteem. I do that simply because I know the power these virtues hold. When you have confidence and self-love, you can conquer the world. Without it, good luck in trying to even conquer yourself. You can be the sexiest and prettiest woman on Earth, but if you don't have the confidence to use your beauty and sex appeal the right way, those gifts will serve you no purpose. Everything we hold, everything we know, and everything we are, are instruments that we can use for either good or bad. We have instruments that we should use to elevate ourselves and the world around us; yet too many people do the opposite.

Confidence creates beauty. Beauty doesn't always create confidence.

I wrote the first version of *Beyond Beauty* at the age of nineteen, and I started my business at twenty. It took a lot of confidence for me to one day wake up and decide that I was going to coach people who were most likely older than I was and had more experience than I had at the time, but I did it anyways. The voices in my head were telling me that I wasn't good enough, that no one would take me seriously, and that there were a lot more coaches out there who had more experience than I had. Most of it was true, but it didn't stop me. I remember how difficult it was at the beginning to go to networking events, conferences, seminars, and other business oriented events knowing that I was the youngest and the least experienced one there. For the longest time I was embarrassed and ashamed to reveal my age.

After watching that interview, I began to use the super model's tip, and soon enough, my results were the same as that model.

Before walking into a room, I would affirm to myself, "I am the most powerful, beautiful, and smart woman in this room." But I wouldn't only say it—I would believe it, I would feel it, I would live it.

When I first started using this technique, I had to fake it, in a kind of playing make-believe "fake it till you make it" way. With time, it became automatic, and I no longer had to think about repeating this affirmation. It would come to me instantly every time I walked into a room, and people responded to it in very surprising ways and reciprocated that energy to me. It became part of my inner affirmations.

It was very surprising the first few times I realized that it was working. I would go to events, conferences, launches, and parties and everyone would want to talk to me. People were drawn to the energy that I was projecting, men were approaching me in a very respectful manner, and people would compliment me not only on my beauty, but most importantly on my knowledge and success.

Everywhere I go, I know for a fact that there will be women who are more beautiful, sexier, and smarter than I am, yet my level of confidence is so strong and powerful that the energy that I project makes it seem as if I was the most beautiful woman in the room, even if that is not true. Remember to consider that the most confident woman in the room is always the most beautiful woman in the room. The way you see yourself is the way people see you.

They say that your thoughts become your reality. I don't think it's necessarily your every single thought that manifests itself into your existence. It's what you believe to be true that manifests itself, therefore if you are a confident woman who knows her worth, who loves herself and who projects feminine essence, it is inevitable—you will be the most beautiful woman in the room everywhere you go. Actually, you are already the most beautiful woman in every space you enter, you just don't know it yet. You've been too busy comparing yourself to other women and their looks but always remember that you can only find your beauty through your confidence, not through your looks.

## A GIFT OR A CURSE

Beauty is a double-edged sword. Just like money, it can be used for good or evil. This does not take away the fact that beauty is a gift that has been given to the world to elevate the energy of love. Beauty is a reminder of love. When you see beauty, whether it be in art, nature, or the eyes of a beloved one, it brings love to the heart, warmth to the soul.

On the other hand, beauty can be deceitful and used for evil purposes. In this day and age, beauty is often used as a manipulative weapon. There are women who sell their beauty for money, attention, and power; there are men who use beauty selfishly and abusively for their own flesh and animalistic desires. Beauty can be a curse, but it is all up to us, the human race, to change this

Our ancestors used to worship beauty, especially the beauty found in nature. They would live for the land; they would nurture it, love it, and respect it. They knew very well that without the beauty of nature and the land they were nothing, so they would care for it, knowing that they belonged to nature and to their motherland. Nowadays, people abuse nature and the land, killing animals, throwing pesticides on the earth and in the skies, destroying forests, and polluting oceans. We are damaging nature's beauty to a point of no return. Contrary to us, our ancestors understood that they belonged to the land. In our own delusion, we believe that the land belongs to us. That's why we now can buy it and sell it, as if we had created it, as if we were there before it was.

The same thing is happening with the human species. Men and women go through plastic surgery to seek the beauty that they fail to see within themselves. We want to change our breasts, our stomachs, our thighs, our arms, even our faces, but in reality it's our spirit that needs a surgery. It is broken, it is damaged. The lack of love that exists in the world doesn't allow us to see beauty and honor it and respect it. Fear is fogging our vision and our hearts; it blinds us from what is really beautiful. We are beautiful, and nature is, art is, children are, animals are, music is, and love is beautiful.

Beauty can definitely be a curse, but only if we allow it to be. You decide what it will be for you.

## USE YOUR BEAUTY

You are Beyond Beauty. You are beyond your physical beauty, beyond your hair, your lips, your hips, and your eyes; you are an eternal being whose light shines so bright that it has the capacity to change the world. What is within you is the most powerful instrument that this universe knows, and you can choose to use it in a positive and purposeful way. If you do, you have the ability to change the course of history. I said it at the beginning of this book, and I'll say it again: This is a defining time in history. It's exciting, yet urgent, it's moving, yet inevitable. We are living at the dawn of a new era. Together, as feminine and beautiful women, we can create this new beginning that will be filled with love, peace, and eternal beauty. We have been called to this mission and to accomplish it, we must use our own beauty.

As women, many of us are born beautiful. Our physiology, the curves of our body, our soft skin and luscious hair are inspiring to men. The greatest literature, art, and music were inspired by women. We are the muse of creation. When a man is interested in a woman, he is often initially attracted to her beauty, which inspires him to love. Love is a contagious energy and if you use your beauty to create love, it will propagate.

Unfortunately, our beauty is often misused for personal gain, whether it is for materialistic, egoistic, or other superficial values. With social media and its followers, young women of this generation are encouraged to use their beauty for these reasons. It's a shame because on places like Instagram, I often see many lovely young women who were blessed with great beauty yet use it only to get attention. They don't know that beauty is a gift, and they were given that gift to inspire the world and bring more love to it. If we don't know how to value and use our beauty the right way, we will not inspire love. We will instead inspire only lust and exploitation.

Think about it—think of all your past relationships or your dating experiences. Do you feel like you are constantly attracting men who don't love you, but just have lust for you? If the answer is yes, it is simply because you are not using your beauty the right way.

A woman's internal and external beauty is meant to inspire love; it is not meant to feed the ego. If we use our natural beauty in this way it is wasted.

There is nothing more beautiful than a woman who lives in her feminine essence, who embodies the Goddess and the Queen. When you know this to be true, you shine, you bring light to the world. Your beauty becomes an instrument of empowerment and inspiration.

As women, we must teach love to men and to do this we use our beauty. We must teach men and the next generations to come how to love like a mother loves her child, that unconditional, all-encompassing love that can heal the universe and repair all faults and wrongs that the people who came before us created. It is no coincidence that a woman can be so attractive to the eye and other senses. With her softness, her femininity, her sensuality, her body and curves, her luscious hair and sweet smile, the arch in her back and the stars in her eyes, the woman was created to inspire love in a man's heart so that he could at once learn how to love.

When a woman is not aware of her gifts and doesn't know of her power, she doesn't use it wisely. She takes her beauty and parades it in a tasteless and ostentatious way. She doesn't honor her body and doesn't care for her womb. Little does she know that her beauty is going to waste, that it is being used and abused for the sake of evil and fear and not for good and love.

Put yourself on a pedestal, and your beauty in a shrine. Use it in a way that is selfless and that will change the world as we know it. This is our time, queens—our beauty is ready to shine.

Every morning, as I get ready for the day ahead of me, I listen to my favorite poem of all time, it's written by Maya Angelou and it's called "Phenomenal Woman."

What the first verse of her famous poem means to me is that a woman's true beauty has little to do with her physical appearance. It is about her inner radiance. No matter what age, race, or body type she has, the true beauty of a woman can be found within herself in her ability to love herself, others, and life. That's what creates her beauty, it's love that creates her beauty in the world. It's also her strength, and yet at the same time, her soft sensuality and femininity. It's her passion and at the same time her warmth and care.

I once read that women are like the ocean—the waves are our constant and passionate emotions and our great power. We are uncontainable, we are constantly flowing, and at our best, we are flowing in love. We are here to generate more feelings of love in the universe. It is our mission.

A phenomenal woman knows her self-worth, embraces her femininity, loves fearlessly, and has full confidence in herself and in the future. It is inside of all of us that the greatest mysteries of the universe hide, and where the most powerful forces on Earth reside. By simply changing ourselves, we can change the entire world. That's how powerful and valuable we all are.

So my message to you, who are beyond beautiful, is to love. Love always with an open heart and don't ever allow anything or anyone to close it for you because that would be you going against your true nature. By loving you will create more beauty, by creating more beauty you will create more love. It is the divine flow in which you must partake. It's what you were chosen to perform as a woman. Being beyond beautiful means to choose to always live in love because that's what you are.

# About the Author

Photograph © Barry MacLeod

**ALEXANDRA VILLARROEL ABREGO** is a trilingual certified life coach, author, international speaker, and businesswoman. Through her work, she teaches women how to unleash their true potential, gain real confidence in themselves, and find a balance between their personal and professional lives so that they may finally live the life of their dreams.

Since the release of her first self-published book in 2010, Alexandra has been giving conferences nationally in her native Canada internationally in North America, South America, and Europe in three languages (French, English, and Spanish).

In 2012 Alexandra was chosen as the national role model for the Hooked on School High School Tour, an initiative of the Ministry of Immigration and Cultural Communities of Quebec, in collaboration with the Montreal Hooked on School organization.

Besides her live seminars and appearances, she also has a very strong presence and following online. Through her weekly online show (AlexandraTV) broadcasted in English, Spanish, and French, she has reached over five million viewers in 134 countries around the world, and counting.

Alexandra is also the founder of A.V.A. Coaching, a consulting and coaching company, which offers an array of world-class personal development and coaching products, programs, and courses for women.

Through her online show, coaching brand, magazine and newspaper articles, training programs, live conferences and new book, Alexandra is quickly becoming a new role model for this generation of young women.